"This is an important book that ... of real-world experience. I belie ... ...y beneficial addition to help reframe how we think about Christian entrepreneurs. More importantly, it is a book that will help entrepreneurs understand how they can use their entrepreneurial talents and drive to contribute to making the world a better place for all."
Karl Moore, Desautels Faculty of Management, McGill University, recently ranked among the world's greatest business thinkers by *Business Strategy Review*, published by the London Business School

"Today more than ever we need Christian entrepreneurs who impact every area of society for the kingdom. Rick Goossen and Paul Stevens have provided a tremendous resource that not only envisions entrepreneurs but also provides practical insights built on a solid biblical foundation. Applying the principles in this book, leaders empowered by the Holy Spirit can change the world."
Geoff Tunnicliffe, CEO/secretary general, World Evangelical Alliance

"When entrepreneurship and authentic Christianity converge, the impact is almost always transformational. We see this in history and we see it today, all over the world. As this book represents that convergence, prepare for the transformational mission to which you'll be called!"
Peter S. Heslam, Transforming Business, faculty of divinity, University of Cambridge, UK

"At last, public policy, business, academic and church leaders are beginning to come together to explore the pivotal role that entrepreneurs play in value creation and societal well-being. For decades, Rick Goossen and Paul Stevens have been at the forefront of empowering such conversations, bringing together diverse communities to explore the creative and redemptive nature of work in all of life's settings. I can think of no better guide to assist Christian entrepreneurs in their mission-critical journey."
John R. Terrill, director of the Center for Integrity in Business, Seattle Pacific University

"Wow! *Entrepreneurial Leadership* is chock-full of wisdom, insight and provocative spiritual sidebars. Don't speed-read this gem—you'll miss the meat. Goossen and Stevens don't just plow new ground—they dig deep. Their harvest is rich with meticulous and fascinating research from real-life entrepreneurs. I was sobered and convicted, then inspired. The risk-taking God. The temptations of reward-seeking. Five misunderstandings of calling. Managing your own ego. Why entrepreneurs struggle with church. It's all there—and more. It's an entrepreneurial feast. I'm buying a case of books for my entrepreneurial colleagues and the pastors who don't get it—yet!"
John Pearson, author of *Mastering the Management Buckets: 20 Critical Competencies for Leading Your Business or Nonprofit*

"The church has long had an uneasy relationship with businesspeople. Too often entrepreneurs are regarded as second-class Christians, useful only for their financial contributions to fund the 'real' work of ministry. That's a shame. And that's why *Entrepreneurial Leadership* is such an important book. It not only counters this dangerous misperception, it equips entrepreneurs with the tools they need to live out their callings for God. Goossen and Stevens are gifted guides, adept at helping Christians understand and practice entrepreneurial leadership. I'll be recommending this book to every business and church leader I know."

Drew Dyck, managing editor of *Leadership Journal*

"This book is critical for the twenty-first-century follower of Jesus. No one has thought more deeply and intentionally than Paul Stevens about the call to be faithful in the places that God locates us. The addition of Rick Goossen's input on entrepreneurial leadership, however, takes it to a new level. The call to be transformative locally and globally is both a practical and thoughtful theological conversation that weaves both the 'Why?' and the 'How?' accessibly. It helps us understand our call. This is a must-read for anyone thinking about faithful and 'salty' living."

Gary V. Nelson, president, Tyndale University College and Seminary, and author of *Borderland Churches*

"There are so many books on leadership in the market that one wonders if there is need for another. However, *Entrepreneurial Leadership: Finding Your Calling, Making a Difference* demonstrates that the topic is far from exhausted. The rigorous, scholarly yet popularly articulated research and ideas of Stevens's and Goossen's book truly command thought and reflection on the part of both established leaders and those just entering the roller-coaster world of guiding and directing others in the pursuit of a large vision. I'm impressed. I think you will be too."

Jim Cantelon, president of Visionledd (www.visionledd.com) and author of *When God Stood Up*

"Evangelicals for much of the twentieth century ignored the political, economic and social marketplace, focusing instead on preparation for a more heavenly world. Goossen and Stevens break out of those fences, leading us to understand the Christ-given gift of the entrepreneur. This comprehensive treatment of Christ-centeredness in the marketplace provides a curriculum, offering wisdom, encouragement and counsel in this vital arena. It is not too much to say this book is an historic breakthrough on a subject too long ignored. I've begun my list of those to whom I will send a copy."

Brian C. Stiller, global ambassador, the World Evangelical Alliance, and president emeritus, Tyndale University College and Seminary

"Richard J. Goossen has been for years speaking to successful entrepreneurs, organizing entrepreneurship conferences and writing on entrepreneurship. R. Paul Stevens has been for years speaking as a marketplace theologian and advocating the integration of faith and work. There are numerous good features in this joint work. I like in particular the quote in the beginning and the mini Bible study at the end of each chapter. The quote points to the key concept in that chapter. The mini Bible study encourages readers to have a biblical foundation to nurture ideas."

Kam-hon Lee, emeritus professor of marketing, The Chinese University of Hong Kong

"Rick Goossen and Paul Stevens have drawn upon many years of experience, reflection and research to craft a thoughtful and truly unique volume. This book should be widely read, as it is brimming with theological and practical insights that apply to entrepreneurial leadership as it is practiced in many settings."

Kenman Wong, professor, Seattle Pacific University, and coauthor, *Business for the Common Good: A Christian Vision for the Marketplace*

"This book is a masterpiece! God's Holy Spirit is infused in Rick and Paul's comprehensive writing and into the perspective that God wants to use us to make a difference for him in our sphere of influence. Reading and applying this book has the potential to change your business and your life—NOW!"

Terry Smith, Smith Gardens, Bellingham, Washington

"Anyone who wants to be his/her own boss—to pursue opportunity and risk responsibility—should think about God as entrepreneur. Goossen and Stevens bring an entrepreneurial God into dialogue with the successful leaders of their research to enrich and enlarge our understanding of what it means to be an entrepreneurial leader and a follower of Jesus in the workplace, the church and the world. This book will make you think about who you are, why you do what you do and how you do it."

Walter C. Wright Jr., former executive director, De Pree Leadership Center, Fuller Theological Seminary

"The partnership of Rick Goossen and Paul Stevens has produced a compelling and useful compilation of theological and practical insights. The book is rooted in the enduring truths of Scripture as well as the lessons learned from interviewing hundreds of Christian entrepreneurs. This will be an encouraging and helpful resource for those who find their calling in entrepreneurship."

Mitchell J. Neubert, Chavanne Chair of Christian Ethics in Business and associate professor of management and entrepreneurship, Baylor University

"I commend Richard Goossen's work because of what he represents as both a practicing businessperson and academic professor. He is himself an entrepreneur; he knows what he is talking about from experience. Yet he is also a careful student, well-read in a variety of areas, including marketplace theology. We need individuals who can straddle the two worlds, who can speak both the language of the boardroom and of the classroom. Such people are rare, but Richard Goossen is one of them. He understands what is necessary to run a successful business and at the same time is mindful of the disciplines of serious academic research."

Richard Higginson, director, Ridley Hall Foundation, Cambridge, UK

"Rick Goossen is passionate about helping Christian men and women rethink how they do business for Christ's sake. The message is clear: God's call on our lives is all-encompassing. Our work life is simply one part of the larger fabric of who and what God calls us to be in the world."

John H. Unger, senior pastor, Ft. Garry Mennonite Brethren Church, Winnipeg, MB

"Rick Goossen is the renaissance man of entrepreneurship. With Canadian and US law degrees, he has the legal knowledge. He founded and runs a business that raises money for entrepreneurs, so he has the financial knowledge. He teaches entrepreneurial skills at the university level, so he has the academic knowledge. And perhaps most importantly, all of Goossen's entrepreneurial knowledge and work is guided by his unique, values-driven view of enterprise. Rick Goossen is an entrepreneur for all seasons."

Larry C. Farrell, chairman of The Farrell Company, Phoenix, and author of *Searching for the Spirit of Enterprise, The Entrepreneurial Age* and *Getting Entrepreneurial!*

"Dr. Goossen is a valuable resource for the church as it deals with what it means to be followers of Christ in our daily work, including the field of business."

Gerald Gerbrandt, president, Canadian Mennonite University

"This book by Richard Goossen and R. Paul Stevens focuses on both the spirituality of being an entrepreneurial leader and the practical aspects of being one. In its ten chapters, the authors first address the essence of entrepreneurship and entrepreneurial leadership, humanistic and Christian models of entrepreneurship, and the meaning and importance of work. The remaining chapters focus on the risks and rewards of being an entrepreneurial leader, finding the right opportunity, aspects of being an entrepreneurial leader and making a difference. By uniquely addressing both aspects clearly and concisely with examples, it is a must-read for anyone starting or already involved in a Christian activity. The book equips individuals from all walks of life to be the entrepreneurial leaders so needed in today's world."

Robert D. Hisrich, Garvin Professor of Global Entrepreneurship and director, Walker Center for Global Entrepreneurship, Thunderbird School of Global Management

RICHARD J. GOOSSEN
AND R. PAUL STEVENS

ENTREPRENEURIAL
LEADERSHIP

Finding Your Calling, Making a Difference

IVP Books

An imprint of InterVarsity Press
Downers Grove, Illinois

InterVarsity Press
P.O. Box 1400, Downers Grove, IL 60515-1426
World Wide Web: www.ivpress.com
E-mail: email@ivpress.com

InterVarsity Press® is the book-publishing division of InterVarsity Christian Fellowship/USA®, a movement of students and faculty active on campus at hundreds of universities, colleges and schools of nursing in the United States of America, and a member movement of the International Fellowship of Evangelical Students. For information about local and regional activities, write Public Relations Dept., InterVarsity Christian Fellowship/USA, 6400 Schroeder Rd., P.O. Box 7895, Madison, WI 53707-7895, or visit the IVCF website at www.intervarsity.org.

All Scripture quotations, unless otherwise indicated, are taken from the Holy Bible, Today's New International Version™ Copyright © 2001 by International Bible Society. All rights reserved.

While all stories in this book are true, some names and identifying information in this book have been changed to protect the privacy of the individuals involved.

Cover design: David Fassett

Interior design: Beth Hagenberg

Images: © Mikhail Mishchenko/iStockphoto

ISBN 978-0-8308-3773-1

Printed in the United States of America ∞

Library of Congress Cataloging-in-Publication Data
A Catalog record for this book is available from the Library of Congress.

P	19	18	17	16	15	14	13	12	11	10	9	8	7	6	5	4	3	2	1
Y	29	28	27	26	25	24	23	22	21	20	19	18	17	16	15	14	13

Contents

Introduction

This book is for you. Perhaps you do not think of yourself as an entrepreneur, or even a leader, for that matter. But you are or can be one. Or you already think you are a leader and are deeply immersed in creating a new business or a new not-for-profit, possibly even planting a church, and feel you may not have time to read this book. But there is much to be gained in reflecting on entrepreneurial leadership and not just giving it. Our conviction in writing this book is that everyone has a calling to make a difference, and everyone has leadership potential whether with a small or large number of people. The world desperately needs entrepreneurial leadership. So read on.

Our desire in writing this book is to equip present and future *entrepreneurial leaders* (defined in chap. 1) to fulfill their God-given entrepreneurial potential. Entrepreneurial leaders need to become equipped if they are to have a transformative impact locally and globally in their respective spheres, whether business person, social worker, factory worker or pastor. In this volume we trust that you will find both how-tos and how-comes. There are lots of books that deal with the how-tos but not many that combine how-to with how-come. Indeed we believe this is the only one that does so with respect to Christian entrepreneurial leadership. This book will help individuals understand their calling both in immediate circumstances and in larger contexts. We will explore both the inside (the spirituality) of being an entrepreneurial leader as well as the outside (the practice and issues around being a leader). So there are chapters that deal with practicing and sustaining entrepreneurial leadership.

Look at the table of contents. We start by describing the essence of being an entrepreneur. Then we talk about leadership both from the standpoint of mainstream literature and from a biblical perspective. We tackle the important issue of fusing entrepreneurship and leadership into the powerful notion of Christ-inspired entrepreneurial leadership. Then in chapter three we consider entrepreneurship with and without God by contrasting humanist and Christian perspectives. In this book we approach the subject from a Christian perspective, but we believe that people with different starting points can profit from these reflections. The business and entrepreneurial community, as reflected in literature and educational institutions, is interested in values-based approaches to the marketplace. We get inside the entrepreneur in chapter four as we consider the soul and spirituality of being an entrepreneurial leader. Next we examine meaning and work ethic to uncover the root of why we do what we do. We then take a biblical perspective on risk versus reward. Chapter seven examines the notion of finding your calling, which we regard as the rudder of the ship of life. With this framework in place we then draw on our extensive research, described in the following section, to summarize the seven most common principles for successfully practicing Christian-based entrepreneurial leadership. There are of course challenges faced by entrepreneurial leaders. Chapter nine lists seven principles for sustaining entrepreneurial leadership. All of this leads us to focus on how you can make a Christ-inspired difference in your various spheres of influence, not just now but on an ongoing basis. But why have the two of us taken up this challenge?

The two of us, Rick Goossen and Paul Stevens, were drawn to collaboration because we believed our complementary strengths would produce a thorough and balanced book. Although trained in law, I (Rick) have been involved in entrepreneurial pursuits for the bulk of my professional career. I have been a founder, director, officer and adviser to numerous entrepreneurial and early-stage companies in North America and Asia. I work full time advising and partnering with successful entrepreneurs. In addition I have taught at universities, spoken at churches and conferences and written books. I am presently director of entrepreneurial leadership, Transforming Business, University of Cambridge (transformingbusiness.net). For over twenty-five years I have wrestled with the challenges of applying the Christian faith in an entrepreneurial context.

I (Paul) grew up in a business family and worked in my father's steel-fabricating business for several years. I was trained in theology and have been a pastor of churches in both the inner city and in the university, worked as a student counselor, apprenticed as a carpenter, owned and run a construction business, and for the last two decades served as a marketplace theologian, which is simply the integration of faith and work. In all of these contexts I have brought some creativity and innovation. More recently I have been teaching not only at Regent College in Vancouver but more widely in Asia, North America and other parts of the world. In the course of this I have spent time in the workplaces of friends and acquaintances and published my findings in several books.[1] We believe we both bring rich research and wide experience to this book.

The Research Basis of the Book

I (Rick) desired to learn from the experiences of other entrepreneurs who shared my same evangelical Christian perspective—but was unable to find much valuable material. This lack of resources and guidance led me to conduct my own research, at first merely to supplement my own entrepreneurial experiences and faith journey. I began formalized primary research in 2004 while an adjunct professor at a Christian university. I constructed a series of questions relating to entrepreneurship and faith, which I refer to as the "Entrepreneurial Leader Questionnaire" (ELQ).[2] Along

---

[1]*The Other Six Days: Vocation, Work and Ministry in Biblical Perspective* (Grand Rapids: Eerdmans, 1999); *Doing God's Business: Meaning and Motivation for the Marketplace* (Grand Rapids: Eerdmans, 2006); with coauthor Alvin Ung, *Taking Your Soul to Work: Overcoming the Nine Deadly Sins of the Workplace* (Grand Rapids: Eerdmans, 2010); and *Work Matters: Lessons from Scripture* (Grand Rapids: Eerdmans, 2012).

[2]The ELQ can be found as an appendix in Richard J. Goossen, ed., *Entrepreneurial Leaders: Reflections on Faith at Work*, 5 vols. (Langley, BC: Trinity Western University, 2007–2010), 5:241-50. The ELQ can also be accessed online at www.eleaders.org/

with students under my direction, I have been able to interview approximately 250 entrepreneurs and compile extensive research data on the intersection of Christian faith and entrepreneurship (referred to as the "Entrepreneurial Leader Research Program" [ELRP]).[3] In addition, a number of esteemed professors have assisted in this research by conducting interviews.[4] From 2004 to the present entrepreneurs from throughout Europe, Africa and North America have been interviewed. Please note that when we refer to the individuals interviewed as part of the ELRP, we refer to them as Entrepreneurial Leaders, and when we generalize to the broad group we use the noncapitalized form of entrepreneurial leaders. I should point out that although the ELRP was conducted by me and I refer to myself as having conducted the research in various parts of the book, the conclusions presented in this book

---

qry/page.taf?id=113. The original questionnaire was inspired partially by an entrepreneur interview exercise included in Jeffry A. Timmons and Stephen Spinelli, *New Venture Creation: Entrepreneurship for the 21st Century*, 7th ed. (New York: McGraw-Hill/Irwin, 2007), pp. 29-31, which was then modified for my research purposes. I focus on people who identify themselves as Christians, who believe in the Bible as God's revealed Word to show us who God is and what God's purpose is for humankind, and who are convinced that God's desire is to bring transformation to people, to society and to all creation.

[3]I refer to this body of work, which is ongoing, as the Entrepreneurial Leader Research Program. The ELRP is a useful starting point, but is limited by the particular parameters within which the research was undertaken. First, the focus was largely on a Protestant evangelical perspective on integrating faith in an entrepreneurial context. Second, the conclusions are based on a limited pool of Christian entrepreneurs and thus must be assessed accordingly. However, the research has proven to be valid. The questionnaire focuses on general entrepreneurial questions and a separate section on faith in the marketplace. The responses to the general entrepreneurial questions are consistent with academic research (i.e., the role of business plans, financing, etc.). The ELRP resulted in a number of publications. I have edited a selection of interviews with entrepreneur leaders on a semi-regular basis: the first two under the title *The Christian Entrepreneur: Insights from the Marketplace* (2005, 2006) and the last three under the title *Entrepreneurial Leaders: Reflections on Faith and Work* (2007, 2008, 2010; all published by Trinity Western University, Langley, BC, Canada). This ongoing research provides valuable and unique insights as to how entrepreneurs practice their faith. This book will quote from individual Entrepreneurial Leaders throughout.

[4]One professor is my colleague Dr. Peter S. Heslam, who heads a research center called Transforming Business at the Faculty of Divinity, University of Cambridge (www.transformingbusiness.net). Another interviewer is a mutual friend of Paul and me, Dr. Richard Higginson, director of faith in business at Ridley Hall Foundation, Cambridge, UK, who has conducted interviews and has delved into the topic through organizing a seminar at Cambridge and in various writings (www.ridley.cam.ac.uk/fib.html).

are those of both Paul and myself.

How was this research conducted? I used the ELQ to obtain detailed firsthand stories from the participant's perspective. In order to provide valuable insights the focus was on entrepreneurs with many years of experience who are most likely to be able to reflect effectively on their own experiences.[5] The emphasis was on factual questions relating to *what* and *how* rather than analytical (*why*). In short, the focus was on how entrepreneurs think and why they act the way they do, rather than asking them to analyze the process.

The ELRP has also led to a larger movement to connect, equip and inspire Christian entrepreneurial leaders worldwide. When I published the first collection of interviews with Entrepreneurial Leaders, I decided to organize a book launch and to publicly acknowledge the support of the interviewees. To my surprise this book launch—which was promoted by word of mouth only—was able to attract two hundred attendees. This book launch has evolved since that time to become the "Entrepreneurial Leaders Conference," which is widely acknowledged as the leading event of its kind to equip, connect and inspire Christian entrepreneurial leaders for global impact. These live and videocast conferences have been attended since inception by thousands of entrepreneurs from throughout North America and worldwide. The annual Entrepreneurial Leaders Conference is now organized through a nonprofit ministry I founded, which is called the Entrepreneurial Leaders Organization (ELO) (eleaders.org).[6] The ELO is supported by a board of entrepreneurs and educators including Paul Stevens, who is an adviser and theological referee. In addition to

---

[5]Donald Schon explains that the most useful information is derived from practitioners who experiment, reflect and then come to viable conclusions and continually refer back to prior experience. See Donald Schon, *The Reflective Practitioner: How Professionals Think in Action* (London: Temple Smith, 1983).

[6]See an overview of ELO in Richard Higginson, *Faith, Hope and the Global Economy: A Power for Good* (Nottingham, UK: Inter-Varsity Press, 2012), pp. 51-53; and Debra Fieguth, "Meet Some of Canada's Marketplace Missionaries: Entrepreneurs and Christian Thinkers examine how their faith relates to business," *Faith Today*, May-June 2012, pp. 19-27.

the conference, Paul and I engage in regular public speaking on various aspects of a Christian foundation for entrepreneurial leadership. The focus of these activities is to empower Christians to utilize entrepreneurial leadership so that they—and you—can fulfill their potential in all facets of life.

I (Paul) have been doing research in a different direction. My passion for five decades has been to connect faith and work, faith and life. To that end I have conducted seminars, preached sermons, written books and even created my own business. This research has been undertaken on several continents, in different cultures and often in one-to-one interviews and immersions in various businesses and enterprises.[7] I am convinced that the Bible and Christian tradition are an amazing resource in understanding the meaning of and motivation for establishing a business or a not-for-profit, or bringing innovation to an existing organization. To that end I have published books on marketplace theology, taking your soul to work, connecting Sunday and Monday, and most recently a book that scours the Bible from Genesis to Revelation on the subject of work. There is a rich tradition historically, theologically and philosophically on connecting faith and enterprise.

Terminology

We need to clarify why we use the term *entrepreneurial leader* and why we do not use the term *Christian entrepreneur*. While this may appear to be a distinction without a difference, there are some important ramifications. The term *Christian entrepreneur* appears to put too much weight on the fact that someone is a Christian and then also an entrepreneur. It will be obvious as we explore various aspects of entrepreneurial leadership that people of faith are going to approach their challenges differently. That will be the subject of several chapters. And yet, having said that, we confess

---

[7]Many of my books have been translated into other languages and one was coauthored with an Asian, Alvin Ung. For further resources go to my website at www.rpaulstevens.com.

that God is at work in people who do not claim to have Christian faith. Often their ethics and work style match or even exceed that of people who claim to be Christians. We have already proposed that in exploring entrepreneurial leadership from the perspective of Christian faith, we are not excluding insights and perspectives that may come from other faith traditions. And we are anxious to show that many aspects of entrepreneurial leadership are common both to people of faith and people without faith. While we may occasionally use the term *Christian entrepreneur*, a more precise approach is to speak of the individual as an entrepreneur who is a Christian. Further, why do we use the term *leader*? In chapter two we explain the importance of using the term *entrepreneurial leader* rather than simply *entrepreneur*.

How to Use This Book for All It's Worth

So that is what this book is about. But how you use the book can be tailor-made for your own situation and your own work style. You may wish to simply read a chapter each day. Most chapters take about twenty minutes. In two weeks you will have read the entire book. You can even pick and choose the chapters, though they do follow a sequence that is thoughtful and connected. At the end of each chapter are discussion and reflection questions. You can use these by yourself in a daily time of reflection or when you are having a coffee break. But if you are meeting for a vocational support group or a downtown discussion group, you could assign a chapter to be read in advance, and when you meet these questions can become the basis of your conversation. There is even a very short Bible study at the end of each chapter. This involves reading a brief portion of Scripture and then engaging the text and letting the text engage you through the one or two questions that are offered. For people teaching entrepreneurship, marketplace ministry or innovation, whether in a business school, a theological school or a pastor's study group, this book can become a textbook. For more in-depth study, readers can access interview transcripts and video interviews at www.eleaders.org.

Back to our underlying purpose: Our desire is to equip present and future entrepreneurial leaders to fulfill their God-given potential. Read, digest and go out and make a difference. And let us know if the book has been helpful in doing just that!

1

The Essence of Entrepreneurship

Not everyone liked the idea. A lot of people said,
"It's a crummy little hamburger stand. How are
you going to make any money out of it?"

GEORGE TIDBALL

This was the response of some people to the launch of McDonald's in Canada. George Tidball was a Canadian doctoral student in economics at the University of Chicago in the early 1960s. His wife came across a small hamburger restaurant where the service was friendly, the place was clean and the food was served very quickly. George could buy a burger and fries for 30 cents. George, his wife and their three kids loved it. The family moved back to their hometown of Vancouver. His wife exclaimed, "This town could really use a McDonald's!" George recognized the opportunities springing from this innovative company in the food service sector. He secured the rights for McDonald's in Canada. His first restaurant opening was a nail-biting experience. George recalled the skepticism toward his nascent business, but he took the risk. George vividly recalled that Thursday morning on June 1, 1967, when he and his financial backers opened the first McDonald's restaurant in Canada: "Shortly before opening, as I contemplated the fact that I had my entire net worth on the line through my personal guarantee, I thought to myself, 'What if no one comes?'"[1] They came—in droves.

---

[1]George Tidball, quoted in *Entrepreneurial Leaders: Reflections on Faith at Work*, ed. Richard J. Goossen (Langley, BC: Trinity Western University, 2007–2010), 3:185.

In fact, even with George's MBA from Harvard he didn't calculate properly the amount of burger patties required. They ran out! George, with his partners, owned and ran McDonald's Canada from 1967 to 1971. They opened thirty-two stores.[2]

Why George? Why was he the one who recognized the opportunity, took the entrepreneurial risk and in the face of criticism from many proceeded down an unknown and unproven path? What is the mindset of this type of person that thinks outside the box?[3] To understand the entrepreneurial mindset is challenging but necessary as a foundation for the subsequent discussion in this book. This book not only describes entrepreneurial leadership but has the objective of equipping you to become an entrepreneurial leader. Further, an understanding of entrepreneurs is related also to the question of whether it can be taught; otherwise this information is of little practical value. We will now address these two interrelated questions.

What Is Entrepreneurship?

One seasoned billionaire entrepreneur who has tasted both disappointment and triumph boldly stated, "I don't think you can teach entrepreneurship. I don't think it's possible. You either have it in you or you don't. There are managers and there are leaders. Entrepreneurship is something I don't personally think you can teach."[4] If anyone is qualified to make such a statement, this particular man is. He was born in 1928, in Saskatoon, Saskatchewan, Canada, but he started working as an entrepreneur in Vancouver, British Columbia. He recounted to

---

[2]Eventually McDonald's US bought back the rights to the Canadian market. George's investors each put in $10,000 in 1965 and received $1 million in 1971. George and his wife together netted $3 million.

[3]Our focus in this chapter, and indeed in this book, is on the entrepreneur rather than the entrepreneurial process. Thus, we are focused on understanding the motivations and thinking of the individual. We prefer the term *mindset* rather than *mind. Mind* implies intelligence that a person is either born with or without. *Mindset*, on the other hand, suggests that the entrepreneurial approach to work and life can be developed, enhanced and improved. See Ian MacMillan and Rita Gunther McGrath, *The Entrepreneurial Mindset: Strategies for Continuously Creating Opportunity in an Age of Uncertainty* (Boston: Harvard Business School, 2000), p. 1.

[4]Jim Pattison, telephone interview with Richard J. Goossen, October 6, 2005.

me (Rick) that one of the most exhilarating times in his life was in 1961 when he started his first business: a two-car showroom with a gas station. Building that business, and the others he has since accumulated, has been a challenge-laden task. He told me, "I've had the bank call my loans a couple times. Those weren't good times. . . . I've had a terrific amount of disappointments."[5] But his zest, determination and undeniable entrepreneurial skills have taken him from the flatlands of Saskatchewan to the peaks of the business world.

He is now in his eighties and is the sole owner of the third-largest privately held company in Canada. He is also involved in a wide range of businesses: automotive, entertainment, export, finance, food, illuminated signs, media, packages and periodical distribution. One of his best-known global brands is *Ripley's Believe It or Not.* Today, he owns the third-largest private company in Canada with $7.3 billion in sales, 34,000 employees and 465 locations.[6]

How does Jim Pattison keep the entrepreneurial spirit alive in his organization? Does he truly believe you can't teach entrepreneurship? Not really. His comment, however, focuses on some of the determinants of entrepreneurship that *are* unteachable—childhood experiences, drive, determination, the chip on one's shoulder, the need to prove one's own worth through accomplishment, and an obsession with money-making opportunities. So, to some degree, people either have it or they don't, and that is proven in the marketplace. Many entrepreneurs simply appear to be hardwired for the passionate pursuit of opportunity.

On the other hand, there are other aspects of entrepreneurship, such as understanding and pursuing innovation, that can be taught and improved. Jim Pattison understands this. To teach his core team of seventy or so executives about entrepreneurship, he has hired entrepreneurship expert Larry C. Farrell to address key issues and teach practical tips.[7] Jim Pattison's comments, then, are not

---

[5]Ibid.
[6]See the Jim Pattison Group's website at www.jimpattison.com.
[7]See "Larry C. Farrell," in Richard J. Goossen, *Entrepreneurial Excellence: Profit from the Best Ideas of the Experts* (Franklin Lakes, NJ: Career Press, 2007), p. 14.

contradictory—though they may seem so at first. Rather, they reveal the nuanced approach that is required to understand entrepreneurship more fully. In fact, his perspective reflects one of the key challenges of discussing entrepreneurship: finding its definition. Until we know what it is, how can we determine how to pursue it?

Many entrepreneurial experts have wrestled with different definitions of entrepreneurship. Howard H. Stevenson, a Harvard Business School professor, notes that there have been two traditional ways of defining entrepreneurship: either as an economic function or as a set of individual traits.[8] The functional approach focuses on the role of entrepreneurship within an economy. For example, the invisible hand of the economy may result in problems that need solutions and an assortment of innovative responses arise to address the need. The other approach, focused on the personal characteristics of entrepreneurs, seeks to compile commonalities in the psychological and sociological aspects of entrepreneurship.

Stevenson finds both approaches unsatisfactory. In his opinion the functional approach correctly highlights innovation but leaves out the process of subsequent exploitation. Conversely, the psychological model is interesting but inconclusive and inconsistent. From Stevenson's perspective, entrepreneurship should be taught—and is indeed taught at Harvard Business School—as a process and not as a personality.[9] Stevenson defines entrepreneurship as the "pursuit of opportunity without regard to resources currently controlled."[10] His definition is broader than that of other experts: it includes the concept of innovation, but also transcends it. The psychological model rooted in the notion that someone is born an entrepreneur, by comparison, may provide some backward-looking insights, but only when the individual has already pursued an opportunity.

Another important perspective is that of Peter Drucker, the father of modern management (who passed away in 2005). In the preface

---

[8]Amar Bhide, H. Irving Grousbeck and Howard H. Stevenson, *New Business Ventures and the Entrepreneur,* 5th ed. (New York: McGraw Hill, 1999), p. 4.
[9]Howard Stevenson, phone interview with Richard J. Goossen, August 8, 2005.
[10]Bhide, Grousbeck and Stevenson, *New Business Ventures,* p. 5.

to *Innovation and Entrepreneurship*, his magnum opus on the topic, Drucker talks about what entrepreneurship is and is not. At the time his book was written (1985), there was still some talk about entrepreneurship being a function of a certain personality type: either you had it or you didn't. Drucker disagreed. The notion of an "entrepreneurial personality type" has been increasingly discounted right through to the present day.

Drucker believed that an entrepreneur can benefit from having certain traits, most of which can be acquired or developed, but that there is no such thing as an entrepreneurial personality. He talked about entrepreneurs in terms of their actions rather than their psychological makeup. Moreover, he explained that his book "presents innovation and entrepreneurship as a practice and a discipline. It does not talk of the psychology and the character traits of entrepreneurs; it talks of their actions and behavior."[11] Of course, if entrepreneurship were the outgrowth of a particular personality, then rather than studying the field in terms of practices and principles the focus would be on psychological predispositions.

Furthermore, Drucker viewed entrepreneurship as a field that can be approached systematically—and, in this way, he saw it as similar to management. His book defines entrepreneurship as "purposeful tasks that can be organized—and are in need of being organized—as systematic work." As well, his writing "treats innovation and entrepreneurship, in fact, as part of the executive's job."[12] In view of Drucker's preeminence as a management guru, he had the ideal foundation from which to compare and contrast the roles of the entrepreneur and the manager.

Drucker's systematic approach clashed with much conventional thought and practical experience prevalent in the 1980s. Entrepreneurs often relish the perverse virtue in "flying by the seat of one's pants," scurrying from one meeting to another and emerging from chaos as an entrepreneurial triumph. Drucker asserted that success

---

[11]Peter F. Drucker, *Innovation and Entrepreneurship: Practice and Principles* (New York: Harper & Row, 1985), p. 247.
[12]Ibid.

may emerge from chaos, but will more likely emerge in spite of it. He posited that innovation and entrepreneurship can—and indeed must—be pursued in a deliberate, thoughtful manner. Furthermore, successful entrepreneurs need to understand, organize and prioritize their tasks. In this sense, tasks are better spread to executives throughout an organization, and should become part of each manager's job.

But what constitutes the core of entrepreneurship that can then be disseminated throughout an organization? Drucker offered this opinion: "Entrepreneurship is neither a science nor an art. It is a practice."[13] At one end of the spectrum, science involves experimentation—testing hypotheses to validate theories that produce predictable results—and this is not entrepreneurship. At the other end, art is an individualistic, subjective process that is impossible to quantify and replicate. Practice, however, is situated between science and art, and focuses on the realities of the marketplace. Indeed, since the knowledge of entrepreneurship is defined by what works and what does not, any discussion of entrepreneurship needs to be backed up by practical experience in the field.

Another perspective is that of Henry Mintzberg of McGill University, one of the world's leading management gurus. Mintzberg, like Drucker, is known for management thinking rather than entrepreneurship. However, though both Mintzberg's and Drucker's perspectives on entrepreneurship are from the context of management strategy and management education, their insights are complementary and powerful. According to Mintzberg, management (like entrepreneurship) "is a practice that has to blend a good deal of craft (experience) with a certain amount of art (insight) and some science (analysis)."[14] If management is a science, then this implies that one may determine a set of laws about it; similarly, if it is a profession, then codified laws should exist. But Mintzberg believes management is, foremost, a craft, with a certain amount of art. And since management is a craft, the learning process involves an emphasis on experience.

---

[13]Ibid.
[14]Henry Mintzberg, phone interview with Richard J. Goossen, September 27, 2004.

Entrepreneurship, like management, is not a profession—there is no official, widely accepted base of knowledge. Unlike lawyers, who learn technical skills within the context of a carefully defined legal system and use specific legal skills within that context, entrepreneurs have no underlying code of guidance. Entrepreneurship is also not a science. Scientists learn from experiments under carefully controlled conditions in which they isolate various elements in order to measure the different outcomes. Their objective is to achieve similar results when conducting a series of repeat experiments. With entrepreneurship, however, the external environment is almost impossible to control. And history does not repeat itself; there may be similarities to past cycles, but there is no exact parallel. As Mintzberg argues, entrepreneurship does not fit into a predictable, scientific model. Like managers, entrepreneurs must develop skills through practice as they explore the nuances of the marketplace and develop a sense of the different dynamics at play. They must learn how to balance themselves in a rapidly fluctuating environment.

With this broad canvas of our discussion of defining entrepreneurship and understanding how a person could learn to be an entrepreneur, we will now focus on the essence of entrepreneurship. This will then provide a reference point as we discuss various dimensions of Christian entrepreneurial leadership.

The Essence of Entrepreneurship

We believe the following five tenets make up the essence of entrepreneurship. These characteristics are almost always found in the entrepreneurial leader and they are essential to what is desperately needed in every human organization.[15]

1. Innovation. We believe that innovation is the sine qua non of entrepreneurship—the ability to do something new, unique and

---

[15]There is a clear bifurcation between academic and trade publications related to entrepreneurship. The academic publications generally have no reference to or discussion of meaning, life goals and spiritual concerns. Trade publications, on the other hand, have these topics embedded in the core of their discussion of entrepreneurship. See Richard J. Goossen, "Entrepreneurship and the Meaning of Life," *Journal of Biblical Integration in Business,* Fall 2004, pp. 21-74.

different and to satisfy a need in the marketplace. While an inventor comes up with ideas, an innovator delivers market-oriented products and services. The role of the entrepreneur is then the pursuit of innovation within the marketplace. The marketplace in a sense pays for innovation—if someone can offer a better, cheaper product, then the rational person will select that product. Walmart, for example, is rewarded by millions of consumers throughout the world for being a highly effective innovator in the sourcing, distribution and retailing of consumer goods. Drucker defines innovation as "the specific instrument of entrepreneurship. It is the act that endows resources with a new capacity to create wealth. Innovation, indeed, creates a resource."[16]

This process can be pursued within large and small organizations. A small business is not necessarily entrepreneurial. The multi-billion-dollar GE Capital, on the other hand, is a highly entrepreneurial organization—although on a large scale.[17] This same analysis applies to the not-for-profit sector. Churches can be innovators with respect to pursuing ministry opportunities. One example is setting up a daycare center in response to needs in the community by taking advantage of unused rooms during the week and introducing the church building and staff to the community. This process can go beyond opportunistic to become systematic. Drucker explains, "Systematic innovation therefore consists of the purposeful and organized search for changes, and in the systematic analysis of the opportunities such changes might offer for economic or social innovation."[18] In short, entrepreneurship should be understood as embodying innovation—and this can occur within big and small organizations, within corporations (this is termed *intrapreneurship*), by small start-ups and in not-for-profit contexts.[19]

---

[16]Drucker, *Innovation and Entrepreneurship*, p. 280.
[17]Jack Welch, with John Byrne, *Jack: Straight from the Gut* (New York: Warner, 2001).
[18]Drucker, *Innovation and Entrepreneurship*, p. 284.
[19]Entrepreneurship is commonly thought of as an individual involved in new venture creation; when innovation is pursued within an existing organization it is often referred to as "intrapreneurship." See Stephen Spinelli and Jeffry Timmons, *New Venture Creation: Entrepreneurship for the 21st Century*, 8th ed. (New York: McGraw-Hill/Irwin, 2009), pp. 279-80.

2. Seizing opportunities. Entrepreneurs recognize, seize and pursue opportunities to innovate in the marketplace. They see change as normal and healthy. They see it as an opportunity, whether the change is in the market, in technology, in delivery modes or in the culture. "The entrepreneur always searches for change, responds to it, and exploits it as an opportunity," says Peter Drucker.[20] Entrepreneurs are participants and not just spectators. One leading entrepreneurship text notes that "to be an entrepreneur is to act on the possibility that one has identified an opportunity worth pursuing."[21]

An entrepreneur is one who creates a new venture and gathers the necessary resources to pursue the opportunity. Joseph Schumpeter viewed entrepreneurship as a process of "creative destruction" in which innovative products continually displace old ones.[22] An entrepreneur without the ability to garner human and financial resources is like a pilot without a plane—there will be neither takeoff nor flight. At the outset of the process this can be difficult. As a result many entrepreneurs begin by so-called bootstrapping. This means that while they cannot attract much capital to a venture that appears highly speculative, they can reduce their own expenses by forgoing salary or reducing their lifestyle costs. They can also obtain resources by generating profit from their company to fuel expansion.

3. Gaining personal satisfaction through innovation. An individual must believe in the value and benefits of the entrepreneurial life, such as independence and being "captain of one's own ship." Larry C. Farrell highlights the importance of "self-inspired behavior" on the part of the entrepreneur.[23] In short, entrepreneurs must have a clear sense of satisfaction and fulfillment in their work.[24] They will not succeed if they do not like what they are doing but are

---

[20]Drucker, *Innovation and Entrepreneurship*, pp. 277-78.

[21]Robert Hisrich, Michael Peters and Dean Shepherd, *Entrepreneurship*, 9th ed. (New York: McGraw-Hill/Irwin, 2013), p. 6.

[22]Thomas K. McCraw, *Prophet of Innovation: Joseph Schumpeter and Creative Destruction* (Cambridge, MA: Harvard University Press, 2007), p. 3.

[23]Larry C. Farrell, *The New Entrepreneurial Age* (New York: Brick Tower Press, 2011), pp. 132-63.

[24]ELQ, question 2. See also ELRP Analysis.

in it only for the money. "Money is almost never the primary motivation for a successful entrepreneur. In fact, most successful entrepreneurs argue that no one can acquire real wealth by pursuing
money exclusively since they will be unwilling to take the financial
risks from which real wealth flows," notes one author.[25] So-called
lifestyle entrepreneurs will choose to pursue a certain business endeavor in spite of limited financial rewards. In other instances entrepreneurs may start a business so that they can focus on a singular
task they enjoy. For example, a creative individual can focus on designing software programs and reach a high level of fulfillment. That
same person may be deterred from working in a larger corporation
where in addition to software design, they are required to take on
other duties, such as management and human resource planning.
But there are risks involved and the entrepreneur has a special approach to that prospect.

   4. Doing risk analysis. No matter how careful the entrepreneur might be, there will always be some level of risk. And this
can never by negated—only analyzed, reduced and managed. An
entrepreneur must have the discipline to conduct sufficient due
diligence before committing resources to an undertaking. An entrepreneur must often "make decisions in highly uncertain environments where the stakes are high, time pressures are immense and
there is considerable emotional investment."[26] A comfortable level
of risk will depend on how much capital is being invested, the size
and timing of the return and the personal life situation of the entrepreneur. One writer summarizes the review of a potential opportunity as a five-stage process: evaluating business ideas, protecting
the idea (patent protections and nondisclosure agreements), cash
flow analysis, market analysis for competitive advantages, and pre-
paring a competitive analysis.[27] In reality this involves a thorough
risk-reward analysis with respect to a proposed business oppor-

---

[25]Joseph H. Boyett and Jimmie T. Boyett, *The Guru Guide to Entrepreneurship: A Con-
   cise Guide to the Best Ideas from the World's Top Entrepreneurs* (New York: John H.
   Wiley, 2001), p. 32.
[26]Hisrich, Peters and Shepherd, *Entrepreneurship*, p. 7.
[27]Jack Kaplan, *Patterns of Entrepreneurship* (New York: John H. Wiley, 2003), p. 7.

tunity. A person who does not understand the importance of cash flow may be a living example of the following cliché: he had money and no experience; afterward he had experience and no money!

5. *Developing entrepreneurial habits.* As noted earlier, there has been a discussion in the relevant literature as to whether there is a so-called entrepreneurial personality—in other words, traits a person is born with rather than those that could be learned.[28] While certain personality traits may be helpful, entrepreneurship is now generally regarded as mainly a collection of skill sets that can be acquired and mastered. According to Stephen Spinelli and Jeffry Timmons, there are six dominant themes that have emerged from what successful entrepreneurs do and how they perform: commitment and determination; leadership; opportunity obsession; tolerance of risk, tolerance of ambiguity and uncertainty; creativity, self-reliance and adaptability; and motivation to excel.[29] All these traits can be acquired. One leading textbook speaks of the "entrepreneurial mindset" and of "habitual entrepreneurs" who have "in common finely honed skills in forging opportunity from uncertainty."[30] These habitual entrepreneurs have five characteristics in common: they passionately seek new opportunities; they pursue opportunities with enormous discipline; they pursue only the best opportunities; they focus on execution; and they engage the energies of everyone in their domain.[31] As a result, most people can pursue entrepreneurship regardless of their personal disposition.

For a significant reason this book is titled *Entrepreneurial Leadership* because without leadership great ideas never become embodied. But at the same time, people that are gifted in coordinating work and workers—managers—also may not be entrepreneurs as they do not bring to their leadership innovation, seizing opportunities and creating. The bottom line is that all of us are endowed by

---

[28]For an example of a personality-oriented approach see Olaf Isachsen, *Joining the Entrepreneurial Elite: Four Styles to Business Success* (Palo Alto, CA: Davies-Black, 1996).

[29]Timmons and Spinelli, *New Venture Creation*, pp. 249-54.

[30]McGrath and MacMillan, *The Entrepreneurial Mindset*, p. 2.

[31]Ibid., pp. 2-3.

our Creator with the capacity to be entrepreneurial and to equip ourselves to be more effective in utilizing those skills.

For Reflection and Discussion

1. We presented the perspectives of three leading thinkers: Howard Stevenson, Peter Drucker and Henry Mintzberg. Which comments of these thinkers resonated with you and why?

2. Think of three entrepreneurs you know. What are their positive characteristics? What are their negative characteristics? Do you think that you cannot have the one without the other? Why?

3. Consider the five elements of entrepreneurship. Which do you find operative in your own life and work? Do you think of these as innate—part of your genetic code—or learned, or both?

Mini Bible Study. Read the creation narrative in Genesis 1:1–2:3. What does this tell you about the world God created? What do we learn about the dignity of the human person? What job description does the human being have?

2

The Essence of
Entrepreneurial Leadership

*True leadership, from a Christian perspective, must be able to
preserve a deep sense of community and avoid fusing the
needs and desires of the people into a collective unity, with
leadership passing over into the role of the Leader.*

RAY S. ANDERSON,
MINDING GOD'S BUSINESS

Chapter one provided an understanding of the essence of entrepreneurship; we will now examine the other half of the title of this book. What is the essence of entrepreneurial leadership?

The Essence of Leadership

Society's concept of being a leader may be associated with individuals in positions of power: a president of a company, a senior pastor of a megachurch or even the president of a country. The reality is that these people may have a very limited scope of leadership; it may be based primarily or entirely on position rather than influence. The ability to have influence is rooted in relationship. In this book we define *leadership* as a relationship of influence in which followership is gained and goals are met. Understood this way even a person who influences a single person is a leader. It is a truism that to some extent everyone is a leader. What do leaders do and how do they influence people and structures? To answer this question we will draw first on contemporary leadership writing and then look at a biblical perspective.

First, good leaders cultivate the culture of a community or organization. It turns out that the culture (identified by artifacts and symbols, values that are cherished, and fundamental beliefs) speaks more loudly than the leader. Walk into any retail store or any church building and within seconds you judge what and who is important in this community and how things are going to be done. The fundamental work on organizational culture has been done by Edgar H. Schein, and I (Paul) have written on it elsewhere.[1] But the leader is in a sense an environmental engineer, reinforcing values, providing symbols and artifacts that visualize those values, and seeing that the fundamental beliefs of the organization are right and appropriated.

Second, good leaders cast a vision for the community or organization. Throughout the Bible we see that this was implemented by good leaders. Moses held up the vision of the glory of God, the Promised Land and a way of life based on God's covenant with his people. Nehemiah held up the vision of rebuilding the wall of Jerusalem and more fundamentally the rebuilding of the Jewish community. The apostle Paul held up the vision of an international, interracial community composed of Jews and Gentiles in which there would be equality, mutuality and interdependence. Jesus, the leader of leaders, held up the vision of the kingdom of God. It was and is his master thought and should be ours as well—God's dynamic rule in all of life bringing shalom, renewal and the transformation of people and all creation.

Third, leaders implement a process by which followership is gained and goals are attained. We mention process because it is not simply a case of commanding or demanding that followers go in a certain direction, though this is too often done. It is process of recognizing the input, concerns and passions that God has given members of a group, along with other leaders in the same community, and working with this. To do this one needs to think systemically (not systematically). In systems thinking, everything is influenced by everything else be-

---

[1]Schein's leading book in this area is *Organizational Culture and Leadership*, 4th ed. (San Francisco: Jossey-Bass, 2010). See R. Paul Stevens, "Organizational Culture and Change," in *The Complete Book of Everyday Christianity*, ed. Robert Banks and R. Paul Stevens (Downers Grove, IL: InterVarsity Press, 1997), pp. 713-18.

cause everything is connected. Paul talked about this in terms of the body of Christ (1 Cor 12:26). And the leader can only lead the process if he or she actually joins the community (or system), which seems perfectly obvious except that it is sometimes not done at all.

Fourth, good leaders implement fairness and justice. This is patently clear from the original apostles in the Jerusalem church who had to deal with daily distribution of aid in that emergency situation. There was unfairness in providing aid to the Hebrew and Greek widows. The apostles dealt with it by appointing seven people to administer the common assets of the primitive church. Significantly the qualities looked for in the seven included being "full of the Spirit," qualities we would want for church leaders (Acts 6:3).

Fifth, leaders exercise stewardship of the gifts and talents of others. They are stewards of these talents and do all they can, organizationally, strategically, administratively and culturally, to draw out the talents and gifts of members of the community. This is called "equipping" in the Bible, and I (Paul) have written extensively on this for church leaders. In *Joy at Work* Dennis Bakke shows how empowering workers to use their gifts and talents is fundamental to a thriving organization and the well-being of workers.[2] This is especially challenging in relationship to the stewardship of power. Insecure leaders keep all power to themselves. Good leaders who are secure in themselves give power away by empowering others. The irony is that when a person does this, he or she does not lose power completely but rather multiplies power and the capacity to empower.

Finally, good leaders make followers into leaders. This is exactly what Jesus did. But not all leaders are entrepreneurial leaders. Entrepreneurial leaders not only influence people and structures so that new products and services are created and delivered, but they integrate innovation and implementation. An entrepreneurial leader is an influencer of positive change. The title of this book is *Entrepreneurial Leadership*, and we will explain that concept in greater detail, building on the foundation of chapter one and much of chapter two.

---

[2]Dennis W. Bakke, *Joy at Work: A Revolutionary Approach to Fun on the Job* (Seattle: PVG, 2005).

A Primer on Biblical Leadership

Among the thousands of books on leadership there is hardly any that deals explicitly with biblical leadership. There are many how-to books, a few books that deal with the character of the leader (something Scripture emphasizes), and a few that describe leaders in the Bible. But most do not contain a theology of leadership. And what is that? A theology of leadership does not deal with how-to but how-come questions. To be a specific, a theology of leadership asks the following questions: (1) Where does leadership come from, and does God give leadership to enterprises as a special gift or through creational investment in persons? (2) Does Scripture provide perspective on how leaders are to function within the purposes of God? (3) What is servant leadership, understood biblically? (4) Are there special challenges in leadership faced by Christians?

1. Where does leadership come from? This critical question is as old as the nature or nurture debate. Is one born a leader, or does God give a special anointing to people as leaders? Or does the situation make the leader? Or is it all of the above? This is similar to our discussion of entrepreneurship in chapter one. Behind the core question is the biblical truth that everyone is fitted by God to have a sphere of influence, great or small, and thus every person is a leader in some sense. And as a leader we all have the capacity to make a difference. We can trace leadership right back to the very beginning of the Bible. The role of leadership is evident in the Genesis narrative of creation when Adam was called to name the animals, and Adam and Eve were called to fill the earth. First, some people are natural or creational leaders. They have a charisma that makes others want to follow them, be with them, learn from them and undertake what goals and purposes the leader embraces. This is from God. But charisma is dangerous if it is not matched with character. Second, leadership is one of the gifts of the Spirit mentioned in the Pauline letters (Rom 12:8). This means that over and above any natural leadership capacity, which to a larger or lesser extent all have, some people receive an anointing that moves their natural and creational abilities a notch further. This obviously can happen in church situations, but Spirit gifts, as we have already said, are not just for the church but for the world.[3] Usually such an anointed leader exercises faith, administration and—as we shall see—stewardship of others' gifts and their own power. Third, leadership is drawn out by cultural and circumstantial factors. Examples of this in the Bible include Gideon and Samuel. Fourth, leaders emerge in a social context as the result of other leaders making leaders out of followers. Dietrich Bonhoeffer says, "The group is the womb of the leader."[4] In the Bible John 21 tells the story of how Jesus, after his resurrection, empowered Peter to "feed his sheep," making a follower into a leader. This is also what leaders in all kinds of organizations should do. And this too is from God. It is God's purpose as beautifully expressed in Ephesians 4:11-12.[5] It is all from God, including situations in God's providence that draw out leadership.

So, where does leadership come from? From God directly in the personality of an individual, from God through Spirit-gifting, from God in providential circumstances that draw out leadership and from empowering leaders who follow God's purpose of multiplying capacity.

2. What do leaders do? The Bible gives us many examples of good and bad leaders and what they did. On the bad list are King Saul, Diotrephes ("who loves to be first" [3 Jn 9]) and even King Solomon, who enslaved the nation for his own grandiose projects, with the result that his slave master got assassinated and on Solomon's death the nation divided and started a civil war. (Solomon and his inability to finish his life well are discussed in chapter ten.) On the good list are people like Nehemiah, Daniel, David, Paul and Jesus.

As a model leader Jesus exercised leadership (1) life to life—in the context of eating, sleeping, walking, working and engaging in contro-

---

[3]See Miroslav Volf, *Work in the Spirit: Toward a Theology of Work* (New York: Oxford University Press, 1991).

[4]Dietrich Bonhoeffer, *No Rusty Swords*, trans. John Bowden (London: William Collins, 1965), pp. 186-200.

[5]See R. Paul Stevens, *Liberating the Laity* (Downers Grove, IL: InterVarsity Press, 1985); R. Paul Stevens, *The Equipper's Guide to Every-Member Ministry* (Vancouver: Regent College Publishing, 2000), and R. Paul Stevens, *The Equipping Pastor: A Systems Approach to Empowering the People of God* (Washington, DC: Alban Institute, 1993).

versies; (2) situationally—through doing different things in different situations, whether facing conflict or encountering human need; (3) through empowerment—giving away everything he had to his followers and commissioning them to continue his work; (4) through concentration—by focusing on Twelve so that the crowd could ultimately be helped; and (5) by attending to his own needs—through sometimes deliberately dismissing the crowd and even his disciples to spend time with his Father. Jesus served his followers—as vividly demonstrated by his washing their feet and ultimately laying down his life for them.[6] But we need to get behind not only the good examples but the great purposes of God in Scripture to discover what good leaders do.

3. What does servant leadership mean biblically? The seminal treatment of the concept of servant leadership was stated by Robert Greenleaf, who proposed that the best leaders set out to serve others and through this become leaders.[7] Unfortunately, the concept of servant leadership is often misunderstood to mean that leaders should do whatever they are asked and told by followers, making them doormats. Taking the best viewpoint in secular literature, servant leaders meet the real needs of followers and care for their well-being and advancement. They are not primarily serving themselves but the community. Consequently the profound book by Peter Block, *Stewardship*, has the subtitle *Choosing Service over Self-Interest*.[8] But these books, while containing crucial perspectives, miss one essential point theologically. Leaders are first of all called to serve God.

In the four servant songs of Isaiah, a prophetic vision of leadership that was actually fulfilled in Jesus, the leader is called variously "the servant of the Lord" or, when God speaks in the first person, "my servant."[9] That is, the first person the leader serves is the living God. A servant is someone at the disposal of another to do

---

[6]The classic treatment of this is A. B. Bruce, *The Training of the Twelve* (published by Logos Divinity Library, available online at www.trinitytheology.org).

[7]Robert Greenleaf, *Servant Leadership: A Journey into the Nature of Legitimate Power and Greatness* (New York: Paulist Press, 1977).

[8]Peter Block, *Stewardship: Choosing Service over Self-Interest* (San Francisco: Berrett-Koehler, 1996).

[9]Is 42:1-9 (the call of the servant); Is 49:1-6 (the vindication of the servant); Is 50:4-9 (the Gethsemane of the servant); Is 52:12–53:12 (the cross of the servant).

the will of another. The leader is at the disposal of God to do what God wants. What God wants is the empowerment and blessing of people, and the development to maturity of the people and the community. So the leader ends up serving God's interests in the people and therefore is a servant of the people, but a servant by giving God-directed leadership. That changes everything. It changes what the leader does (she or he is fulfilling God's wishes and God's purposes). It also changes how the person does it (in accountability to God and recognizing that the ultimate success or failure of their work is vindicated by God even if they feel they have labored and toiled in vain).

4. *What are the special challenges facing a Christian leader?* One special challenge for Christian leaders is to glorify Christ and not themselves. Perhaps the epitome of a good leader who is a servant of God is found in the apostle Paul. Paul was a strong leader, by creation, by gifting and by circumstance, whose primary service was to God. He had a clear and sustained vision. He empowered his followers (read Acts) and he laid down his life for his followers. But significantly and unlike so many people at the top of organizations, Paul was vulnerable. That is another special challenge of a Christian leader. Paul shared his own struggles. He says in 2 Corinthians 3:12-18 that we are not like Moses, who had to cover his face because people could not cope with the passing glow on his face when he came out of the tent of meeting with God. Rather if we are unmasked, if we are looking at Jesus and if we let people know us, we are actually being transfigured from one degree of glory to another. So what people will see is not just ourselves but a fraction of the image of Christ. This is especially apparent elsewhere in 2 Corinthians. In 1 Corinthians we get to see inside a first-century church, and it is not very pretty. But in 2 Corinthians we get to see inside a first-century Christian leader, Paul himself. And what we see through the struggles, the heartaches, the longings and the vulnerabilities is beautiful enough to make us want to follow him, and to follow Jesus as our leader.[10] Commenting on the tendency of

---

[10]Dietrich Bonhoeffer identified the opposite of this in Adolf Hitler. See his *No Rusty Swords*, pp. 186-200.

some leaders to veil their humanity Ray Anderson says,

> True leadership, from a Christian perspective, must be able to pre-
> serve a deep sense of community and avoid fusing the needs and de-
> sires of the people into a collective unity, with leadership passing over
> into the role of the Leader. . . . This shift brings a dehumanizing
> process to those who are being led, and *a veiling of the true humanity
> of the leader.* . . . [H]e becomes "larger than life," an object upon
> which they can project their own individualistic dreams for success
> and desire for power.[11]

So in this chapter we have explored various aspects of the leader
as a person of influence. We have discovered some of the unique
dimensions Scripture brings to the challenge of leadership, both by
examples good and bad and by direct teaching. In conclusion we
affirm that leaders are gifts of God, and their leadership, if expressed
according to the purposes of God and God's glory, is what the world
desperately needs. But we must now consider what it means to be an
entrepreneurial leader.

The Essence of Entrepreneurial Leadership

We advocate the concept of entrepreneurial leadership as a platform
for making a difference. Authors James M. Kouzes and Barry Z.
Posner, speaking about entrepreneurial leadership, note, "Leaders
are pioneers—people who are willing to take risks, to innovate and to
experiment in order to find new and better ways of doing things."[12]
One entrepreneurship scholar, Ian MacMillan, discusses entrepreneurial leadership and notes that it includes both "transformational
enactment" (envisioning possible outcomes in the face of uncertainty)
and "cast enactment" (motivating large numbers of people).[13] In his
view, entrepreneurship is all about leading and motivating people.

---

[11]Ray S. Anderson, *Minding God's Business* (Grand Rapids: Eerdmans, 1986), p. 79, ital-
  ics added.
[12]James M. Kouzes and Barry Z. Posner, quoted in John C. Maxwell, *The 5 Levels of Leadership: Proven Steps to Maximize Your Potential* (New York: Center Street, 2011), p. 199.
[13]Ian MacMillan, "What Makes a Good Entrepreneurial Leader? Ask Middle Managers,"
  Knowledge@Wharton, April 25, 2001, http://knowledge.wharton.upenn.edu/article
  .cfm?articleid=347.

One of the few references we found on this topic from a Christian perspective was Bill Hybels's brief discussion in *Courageous Leadership* about an "entrepreneurial leadership style"—combining the two concepts, as we have done.[14] Hybels, the well-known pastor of Willow Creek Church, is not, of course, a specialist in entrepreneurship, but provides some useful commentary on how entrepreneurial creativity adds an important dimension to leadership.

One leading entrepreneurship text of the past three decades, authored by Timmons and Spinelli, explains that effective entrepreneurial leaders must be skillful at managing conflict, building teamwork and consensus, and understanding when change is needed.[15] After listing a range of skills and competencies for new venture success, they then list a number of entrepreneurial leadership skills specifically: stakeholder management, the ability to solve problems, the ability to communicate effectively and clearly, the ability to plan, the ability to make decisions on the basis of incomplete data, project management skills, negotiating skills, the ability to manage outside professionals and personnel administration.[16] All these skills and competencies are important, but entrepreneurs' success will be greatly determined by what are conventionally viewed as leadership skills: the capacity to lead, inspire and persuade key people with their vision of the company and its potential.

An entrepreneurial leader is one who pursues opportunities in the face of opposition or limited resources and brings together the human and financial resources necessary to pursue an objective. The focus of our research is not on entrepreneurial activity generally, but rather on entrepreneurs as people who founded ventures from scratch and built them up over time. These are often the types of entrepreneurs that we read about in the media, rather than lifestyle entrepreneurs, social entrepreneurs or intrapreneurs.[17] These

---

[14]Bill Hybels, *Courageous Leadership* (Grand Rapids: Zondervan, 2002), pp. 151-53.
[15]Stephen Spinelli and Jeffry Timmons, *New Venture Creation: Entrepreneurship for the 21st Century*, 8th ed. (New York: McGraw-Hill/Irwin, 2009), p. 319.
[16]Ibid., pp. 315-19.
[17]Lifestyle entrepreneurs are individuals who pursue an entrepreneurial venture pri-

entrepreneur founders reach high levels of success by focusing on innovation and successful marketplace implementation. These entrepreneurs are indeed leaders in that they influence various circles of people, from those within the company to outside stakeholders such as suppliers and customers. These entrepreneurs can magnify their ability to make a difference through understanding not only entrepreneurship but leadership, and how the two work together.

To understand how entrepreneurial leadership can thrive we will draw on the work of John C. Maxwell, one of the world's leadership experts. Maxwell is a long-time pastor who has written a number of widely read books on leadership and is in demand as a key speaker on the topic. Maxwell has constructed five levels of leadership in which he artfully summarizes how the different levels can dramatically expand a person's influence. Level 1 leadership is based on "position"; people follow because of the leader's title. They have no choice. Positional leadership is based on "rights" granted by position and title.[18] Level 2 is based entirely on relationships, and people follow the leader because they want to. It's not about a title. These leaders develop strong relationships with people. Level 3 is based on "production." At this level, leaders get things done and they produce "results."[19] These leaders become change agents within an organization. Next is Level 4, which is about "people development." Maxwell explains that "Leaders become great, not because of their power, but because of their ability to empower others."[20] The leaders engage in "reproduction"—they are developing other leaders. Level 5 is the pinnacle. Maxwell believes that "Only naturally gifted leaders ever make it to this highest level. . . . They develop people to become Level 4 leaders."[21]

For entrepreneurs, Level 1 means that people follow simply be-

---

marily because of the lifestyle benefits provided, which may include independence, working from home, flexible schedule and being involved in an interesting but possibly not lucrative business. An example would be an individual running a pottery business from home.

[18]Maxwell, *5 Levels of Leadership*, p. 7.
[19]Ibid., p. 8.
[20]Ibid., p. 9.
[21]Ibid., pp. 9-10.

cause the leader is the owner. They may neither like nor respect the leader, but he or she is their meal ticket. Entrepreneurs are sometimes shocked that when their dream starts to fade and the vision does not materialize, all the employees—whom they viewed as their ardent supporters and fans—quickly move on to their next opportunity. No surprise. They only followed because they had to! For entrepreneurs, Level 2 occurs when relationships have been created within the company. This is challenging for entrepreneurs because the company, if not the entire world, revolves around them and their aspirations. These entrepreneurs have used their emotional intelligence to engage in peer-to-peer conversation—not top-down dictates. Entrepreneurs should ask themselves: *Would I be able to act in this way if this person didn't work for me?* Level 3 entrepreneurs get things done. This is where the niche of the company has been successfully identified, the team is working in great synergy and the company is on a growth curve. This is where entrepreneurial leadership sometimes starts to stagnate if new opportunities are not pursued.

Level 4 is about people development. This is particularly challenging for entrepreneurs. Most entrepreneurs are focused on the pursuit of their own dreams rather than those of others. Some entrepreneurs, once they have harvested their business, begin to adopt a mentoring role, but this typically happens once the entrepreneur has left the thrust and parry of business, rather than when they are in the middle of it. So if we rely on mentors who have hit the proverbial home run, then this is slim pickings indeed. Our position is that Christian entrepreneurial leaders need to be more engaged in Level 4 leadership on an ongoing basis. As Maxwell noted, Level 5 leaders are uncommon. However, there are entrepreneurial leaders who should strive to reach that level for maximum impact. Of the Entrepreneurial Leaders interviewed, there are a number who have created a powerful legacy. In this context we may speak of it, as Theodore Malloch does, as spiritual capital in an organization that lives from one generation to the next. Malloch lists a gallery of virtuous companies founded by entrepreneurial leaders, including examples such as Herman Miller, Chick-fil-A and many others.[22]

Our concept of entrepreneurial leadership is based on the potent combination of what constitutes a great leader and what the entrepreneurial spirit brings to that leadership. Entrepreneurs must view themselves more deliberately as leaders and realize that they have great ability to influence others. Likewise, leaders benefit by expanding their influence through their capacity to pursue innovation. This fusion of entrepreneurial leadership can have a great impact within a company and beyond.

A couple of examples will demonstrate the powerful combination of leadership skill with the entrepreneurial spirit. One example of how entrepreneurship and leadership are fused is the experience of Allon Lefever. He got into the business of being an Internet service provider at the start of a high-tech boom. He believed there was a window of opportunity to build a network. He did an initial public offering (IPO) on Wall Street with OneMain.com on March 25, 1999. He raised $215 million in a so-called poof IPO, consolidating and closing on seventeen companies at the time of listing. The stock price opened at $29 and ended the day at $39 for a 30 percent gain. He was on national TV in the United States that night. He explained how he was able to impact others: "I had the chance to influence 1,600 employees in a few years with the values statement that we shared with them. It adds meaning and purpose beyond just having a career."[23] Lefever was not merely providing a service or making money. And it wasn't just about his personal calling. Instead, it was about the chance as the founder/entrepreneur to positively influence 1,600 employees with his Christ-inspired set of operational values. Lefever exhibited the characteristics of not only innovating but deliberately influencing his entire workforce.

Another example of an entrepreneurial leader is Graham Power, chairman of Power Group, Cape Town, South Africa. Power has a

---

[22]Theodore Roosevelt Malloch, *Spiritual Enterprise: Doing Virtuous Business* (New York: Encounter Books, 2008), pp. 135-46.

[23]Allon Lefever, quoted in Richard J. Goossen, ed., *The Christian Entrepreneur: Insights from the Marketplace* (Langley, BC: Trinity Western University, 2005–2006), 2:223-24.

one-hundred-year dream for his company. He explains, "It is an undertaking that this company, its culture and ethics will continue to thrive long after our time."[24] This orientation toward the future underscores the strong spiritual side of Power Group. Graham Power explains that this embodies his "personal belief that this [his company] is God's business; not mine or ours. We are merely managing it on His behalf in order to create growth opportunities for our people."[25] He is very conscious of social responsibility and likes to get involved in the communities his company works in, often in extremely disadvantaged areas. Another important aspect of the company is its active involvement in the Global Day of Prayer. Graham Power explains that, "Through a spiritual revival, I am convinced that Africa, which is often referred to as the 'dark continent,' with all the negative sentiments of poverty, unemployment, crime and corruption, prostitution, drug and alcohol abuse and HIV/Aids, will see a major turn-around. I firmly believe God has a plan for Africa, and that we have a role to play in the Transformation of our continent."[26] Power has also initiated "Unashamedly Ethical," a campaign promoting ethics, values and clean living. They facilitate the forming of local Unashamedly Ethical communities all over the world.[27] Graham Power is an excellent example of entrepreneurial leadership in action—combining innovativeness with a desire to make a difference not only in his own country, but around the world.

In the first two chapters of this book we introduced a concept of entrepreneurial leadership. We discussed entrepreneurship in chapter one without raising the notion of spirituality, meaning or God. In chapter two we discussed leadership generally and introduced the powerful combination of entrepreneurial leadership. We also introduced a biblical perspective on leadership—what does the Bible say, if anything, on the topic? We highlighted examples of entrepreneurial leaders such as Allon Lefever and Graham Power, who are motivated

---

[24]Graham Power, "Message from the Chairman," *Power Group,* www.powergrp.co.za/about_message.htm.
[25]Ibid.
[26]Ibid.
[27]See the Unashamedly Ethical website at www.unashamedlyethical.com.

by faith in God to impact not only their businesses but their communities. But how does faith actually make a difference to the practice of entrepreneurship or the concept of entrepreneurial leadership?

For Reflection and Discussion

1. Do you consider yourself a leader? In which ways have you exhibited leadership?

2. Who do you believe are some of the most effective leaders in the Bible and why?

3. In his book *Magnificence at Work*, John Dalla Costa asks some questions of what he calls "kenotic" leaders, that is, leaders who are self-giving and embrace downward mobility like Jesus in Philippians 2. Brood on these.

   - Have we blessed and supported those who have the confidence to "hunger and thirst for righteousness"?

   - Do we have the confidence and imagination to be "merciful" and "pure in heart"?

   - Do we have the audacity to be "peacemakers," and the self-emptying courage to face "persecution for righteousness' sake"?

   - What do we risk to make hope real?[28]

4. Does the idea of being vulnerable and expressing your humanity trouble you? Why?

Mini Bible Study. Read the book of Nehemiah in the Old Testament, especially chapters 4–6. How did Nehemiah deal with opposition and setbacks? What apparently kept him going when the odds were against him? What creative initiatives did he take?

---

[28]John Dalla Costa, *Magnificence at Work: Living Faith in Business* (Ottawa: Novalis, 2005), p. 102.

3

Humanist and Christian Models
of Entrepreneurship

Bidden or not bidden, God is present.

IN CARL JUNG'S STUDY

Is faith in a personal God essential to being an entrepreneurial leader? No, but it makes a difference. If entrepreneurs are a gift to any organization it is because of their in-built passion and abilities (which need to be honed, of course), which are from God, whether or not he is bidden. While we are not proposing that conscious faith in God is necessary to be a vital and successful entrepreneur, we are asserting in this chapter that intentional faith in God makes a difference in terms of meaning and motivation in the marketplace. To explore this we must make an important distinction between two approaches to entrepreneurship. The first, without God, we refer to as the "humanist model" of entrepreneurship; the second, with God, we refer to as the "Christian model" of entrepreneurship.[1]

A Humanist Model of Entrepreneurship

There are three characteristics of the humanist model. And there are also significant results of taking this approach in three areas: the question of human agency, the view of the universe and how one goes about attaining personal fulfillment and success. These are actually questions of worldview.

---

[1]For a detailed discussion of these concepts see Richard J. Goossen, "Entrepreneurship and the Meaning of Life," *Journal of Biblical Integration in Business*, Fall 2004, pp. 21-74.

1. Self-generated personal narrative. In the humanist model each individual creates a belief system through a process of self-discovery unfettered by external doctrine. As Chuck Colson has noted, this type of thinking is attractive for a post-Christian culture because it "assuages the ego by pronouncing the individual divine, and it gives a gratifying sense of 'spirituality' without making any demands in terms of doctrinal commitment or ethical living."[2] Often, however, there is a sense of something beyond mere human society and clusters of individuals. But if there is, as some propose, a divine source of wisdom or global life force, each person has direct access to that source of wisdom—there are no ecclesiastical or organizational impediments. Collective gatherings are used to bless the individual seekers. Each person emphasizes experience rather than doctrine or reference to a transcendent God. The role of an organization is not to reinforce correct doctrine or channel devotion—as in a religious institution—but rather the group simply celebrates their individual experiences. This has implications.

The pursuit of one's personal narrative is, by definition, an eclectic process—choosing from life's buffet of ideas and movements—all geared to self-determined motivations. In some forums *human spirit* is deployed as a generic, inoffensive term to symbolize a pursuit of personal fulfillment. Within an entrepreneurial context the Babson College "Symposium on Spirituality and Business," initiated in 1998, reflects such an approach. I (Rick) experienced Babson's approach when I was a speaker at their symposium in 2005.[3] The director had mentioned to me that they did not have much evangelical Christian participation in their symposium. I soon discovered why as my presentation on the humanist and Christian models of entrepreneurship received a frosty reception. The Babson Symposium captures the nature of the creation of the personal narrative: a journey of dis-

---

[2]Charles Colson and Nancy Pearcey, *How Now Shall We Live?* (Carol Stream, IL: Tyndale House, 1999), p. 264.

[3]Richard J. Goossen, "Entrepreneurship and the Meaning of Life," International Symposium on Spirituality and Business, Babson College, Wellesley, MA, March 22, 2005. Babson College is recognized internationally as a leader in entrepreneurial management education. The tenth symposium in 2007 appears to have been the last one held.

covery without any obligations. They emphasized individualized efforts confirmed by the patina of a respectable academic group hug, but without any overarching doctrine. But the humanist approach has implications for the way we relate to the universe.

2. Mechanistic view of the universe. In the humanist model there is no room for a Creator or external force that may have some bearing on the workings of the universe. This approach has been termed *naturalism*—"the belief that natural causes alone are sufficient to explain everything that exists."[4] In the humanist model this is often referred to as "universal laws." One such law is that wealth can be accumulated by diligent perseverance. Sometimes it is assumed that a supreme spiritual being, if there is one, will bless those efforts. In a syncretistic vein, "laws" from the Bible are sometimes cited, the most common one being "as you sow, so shall you reap." The accumulation of wealth is the chief means by which a supreme being shows its favor with the efforts of humans. Another universal law is the notion that everything will work itself out. For example, "You must have a higher purpose than making money in business. If you have a higher purpose, you marshal all kinds of forces behind you and within you that support you in your goal."[5] One author, using an argument based on "alchemy," goes so far as to say that, "God does want each of us to be rich in every possible way—health, love, and peace of mind, as well as material possessions."[6] We are not told how or why, but simply that we should have these expectations. This view of the universe relates to the drive to become a fulfilled person.

3. Personal fulfillment. A common mantra of the humanist model is that "Business is and will remain the great modern arena for individuals to express their vocation and develop their potential."[7]

---

[4]Colson and Pearcey, *How Now Shall We Live?*, p. 20.

[5]Marc Allen, *Visionary Business: Entrepreneur's Guide to Success* (Novato, CA: New World Library, 1995), p. 29.

[6]Paul Zane Pilzer, *God Wants You to Be Rich: How and Why Everyone Can Enjoy Material and Spiritual Wealth in Our Abundant World* (New York: Simon & Schuster, 1997), p. 14. The ancient alchemists sought to discover the secret of turning base metals into gold.

[7]Colin Turner, "The Spirit of Entrepreneurship" #562, *Innovation Leader* 11, no. 10 (2002), www.winstonbrill.com/bril001/html/article_index/articles/551-600/article562_body .html.

While your purpose may be helping people, your niche will be the mechanical or technical thing you are good at doing. Entrepreneurs will spend a lot of time finding their niche—what they are good at and how their service or good fits into the economy or the organization they serve. One leading writer in this field, Richard J. Leider, explains: "We all have natural abilities and inclinations and find that certain things come easily to us. We may perform a talent so effortlessly that we forget we have it. This is a 'gift.' We were born with it!"[8] There are different ways to discover your niche. One technique is to explore the eight core categories that summarize the talents we each have.[9] Another technique is to use the theory of multiple intelligences: linguistic, logical, spatial, musical, kinesthetic, interpersonal, intrapersonal and naturalistic.[10] The relevance of these skills is that, "Our ability to discover and embrace our unique gifts establishes the power behind our purpose."[11] Some, such as motivational guru Tony Robbins, have called this ability to achieve our own success and fulfillment awakening the giant within us.[12]

This approach to self-fulfillment can be traced back to Abraham Maslow, who attempted to synthesize a large body of research related to human motivation, which became known as "Maslow's Hierarchy of Needs."[13] At the top of the original hierarchy, subsequently modified, was "self-actualization." This highest need is to find self-fulfillment and to realize one's potential without the help of any divine source or guidance. One recent book adopts the same approach to business, but uses slightly different terminology. The authors refer to the highest level of being as the "State of Self-Reliance," which has the following characteristics: "High self-esteem and inner validation. Motivation from within. Following the 'Inner Voice.' Being free from

---

[8]Richard Leider, *The Power of Purpose: Creating Meaning in Your Life and Work* (San Francisco: Berrett-Koehler, 1997), pp. 113-14.

[9]Ibid., p. 115.

[10]Ibid., pp. 116-17.

[11]Ibid., p. 118.

[12]Tony Robbins, *Awaken the Giant Within: How to Take Immediate Control of Your Mental, Emotional, Physical and Financial Destiny!* (New York: Free Press, 1992).

[13]William G. Huitt, "Moral and Character Development," Valdosta State University, 2005, http://chiron.valdosta.edu/whuitt/brilstar/chapters/chardev.doc.

all needs and giving selfless service to others. Experiencing no resistance."[14] Further, this level of being—the state of self-reliance—is part of the "Self-Realization Stage." At this stage, say the authors,

> You are fully conscious and awake, which requires you to demonstrate total integrity in everything you do. This is not easy. Very few people live their lives in this rarefied atmosphere. As you become more aware, you become less attached to events and the need for so many material things. Service to others becomes more important and you experience no resistance.[15]

In short, the power of individuals to look further within, rather than outside themselves, is a core aspect of the humanist model of entrepreneurship. Where does this approach to work, life and entrepreneurship come from?

The Cultural and Philosophical Trends Behind the Humanist Model

The rise of the humanist model is a reflection of the times we live in. The cultural and philosophical trends behind the humanist model are well expressed in popular literature and the media. We will reference briefly five factors that have shaped the humanist model.[16] First, there is the deinstitutionalization of spirituality. Society has drifted toward personalized spirituality and away from religion in an organized and institutionalized sense.[17] This shift in the Western perception of the human person shorn of institutionalized religion can be traced back as far as 1700. Since that time effective public advocates have played a central role in bringing about a new spiritual outlook.[18] A second

---

[14]Jack Canfield, Mark Victor Hansen and Les Hewitt, *The Power of Focus: How to Hit Your Business, Personal and Financial Targets with Absolute Certainty* (Deerfield Beach, FL: Health Communications, 2000), p. 285.

[15]Ibid., pp. 286-87.

[16]For a more detailed discussion see Goossen, "Entrepreneurship and the Meaning of Life."

[17]In the United States, the Gallup Institute polls individuals about the religions and spiritual impact in their lives. See George H. Gallup Jr., "Americans' Spiritual Search Turns Inward" (February 11, 2003), www.gallup.com/poll/7759/americans-spiritual-searches-turn-inward.aspx.

[18]James A. Herrick, *The Making of the New Spirituality: The Eclipse of the Western Religious Tradition* (Downers Grove, IL: InterVarsity Press, 2003), p. 250.

trend is that secular humanism has become the dominant approach to life, at least in the West, and to a large extent globally. Humanism—the belief in humankind only—can be both optimistic and pessimistic. On the latter, the one-time director of the British Humanist Society once said that the most drastic objection to humanism is that it is too bad to be true.[19] Human beings left alone with humans will be worse than beasts. On the optimistic front are those who forecast a future technological paradise and those who believe in the ultimate divinity and endless possibilities of the human spirit. A third trend contributing to the humanist model is postmodernity, which is a way of expressing the new way people now relate to reality. One of the characteristic emphases of postmodernism is that "all universal theories, truth-claims and teleological readings of history—'totalizing meta-narratives,' in the jargon of the day—are obsolescent."[20] The fourth trend is the growth of the "new age" movement, which has been defined as "a spiritual movement seeking to transform individuals and society through mystical union with a dynamic cosmos. Its advocates hope to bring about a utopian era, a 'New Age' of harmony and progress that some say has already begun."[21] The fifth trend, in many ways the product of the first four, is the human potential movement. The central thrust of this movement is that people have the power within themselves to unlock their extraordinary potential. These five societal trends have quite naturally affected how people understand entrepreneurship. Since the soil in which these trends have taken root is devoid of God, the humanist model is consequently quite different than a Christian approach.

A Christian Model of Entrepreneurship

The important distinction between the humanist and Christian models is not typically understood or identified because Christians are prone to

---

[19]Quoted in Clark H. Pinnock, *Set Forth Your Case* (Nutley, NJ: The Craig Press, 1967), p. 17.

[20]Vinoth Ramanchandra, *Gods That Fail: Modern Idolatry and Christian Mission* (Downers Grove, IL: InterVarsity Press, 1996), p. 4.

[21]John P. Newport, *The New Age Movement and the Biblical Worldview: Conflict and Dialogue* (Grand Rapids: Eerdmans, 1998), p. 1.

reflect culture rather than lead it. The outcome we seek to avoid is that of the withered tree with no good fruit. Let's unpack each of the three characteristics of the humanist model and contrast that clearly with a counterpart in the Christian model of entrepreneurship.

By referring to a Christian model of entrepreneurship we do not mean there is a unique set of faith-based techniques to achieve financial success. Instead, the Christian model consists of tenets that provide an intellectual framework—or worldview—from which to approach entrepreneurship. A worldview is "simply the sum total of our beliefs about the world, the 'big picture' that directs our daily decisions and actions."[22] A worldview is the way a person sees reality. In a classic volume on worldview James Sire says,

> A worldview is a commitment, a fundamental orientation of the heart, that can be expressed as a story or in a set of presuppositions (assumptions which may be true, partially true or entirely false) which we hold (consciously or subconsciously, consistently or inconsistently) about the basic constitution of reality, and that provides the foundation on which we live and love and have our being.[23]

Worldview is the story about everything that gives us meaning and helps us make sense of life. It is the way we see everything, the lens through which we view everything and experience life. For the Christian model, this worldview is rooted in the story of the Bible.

The Bible is a story that contains within its grand metanarrative many stories. But essentially it is the story of God's romance with the world and God's unquenchable and gratuitous love for humankind. It is the grand narrative of God's determination to bring his life-bringing rule into all creation and all people, concluding in the transformation of everything into a new heaven and a new earth. As a story it has a beginning, a middle and an end. It is going somewhere. But it is also taking us with it. Because the biblical story is the grand story of who we are, who God is and what it all means, it is a story that catches up our life callings and enfolds them in a grander narrative. And by in-

---

[22]Colson and Pearcey, *How Now Shall We Live?* p. 14.
[23]James Sire, *The Universe Next Door: A Basic Worldview Catalog*, 4th ed. (Downers Grove, IL: InterVarsity Press, 1976), p. 17.

cluding us it changes our way of thinking and behavior. Eugene Peterson comments, "We are immersed in the intricate triangle of
human life as it is entered, addressed, confronted, saved, healed and
blessed by the living God—God's Spirit breathed into human lives."[24]
The Bible is central to gaining a Christian worldview.

Drawing on Sire, a worldview answers several critical questions.
What is real? (Actually, the issue is the really real, not just real,
referring to ultimate reality.) What is the nature of the world?
What is a human being? What happens at death? (Believe it or not,
that is an important issue. If death is the end, or if we get recycled
in a better or worse life, it makes a big difference to what we do in
the world in this life.) Further worldview questions are: Who is in
charge of the world? Can we know anything? How do we know
right and wrong? What is the meaning of human history? The answers to these questions get communicated through the media,
through popular culture, through education, through religious expression and teaching, and through family education. It is like a
dense fog that seeps through everything, right to the bone, and influences values, belief and behavior. For the Christian the answer
comes mainly from the Bible and the tradition of the Jewish and
Christian faith communities. But we cannot always draw a sharp
distinction between the worldviews underlying the humanist and
Christian models.

Part of the challenge in making this contrast is that the humanist
model is similar to the Christian model—albeit in superficial ways.
The Entrepreneurial Leader Research Program, referred to in the
introduction, reveals that Christians practicing entrepreneurship
are unwittingly attracted to and accepting of elements of the humanist model without recognizing the deeper-seated inconsistencies
with their own worldview. The first key difference is the metanarrative that makes sense of all of life. We prefer to use the term *God
narrative* in order to contrast this concept more clearly with the
self-narrative of the humanist model.

---

[24]Eugene Peterson, foreword to Michael Green and R. Paul Stevens, *New Testament
Spirituality* (Guildford, UK: Eagle, 1994), p. viii.

1. A God narrative. This God narrative provides a worldview that is the mental and spiritual infrastructure for how we live and work. Take the first worldview issue for example: What is real? The secular mindset is that there is no god, and matter is what is really real. In some thought perspectives, systems that dominate a whole culture, there is no transcendent personal God. Everything and everyone is divine. In another religious system, God is conceived as absolute will, leaving little room for human initiative. In an animistic culture, the spirit world is more real than the material world, making entrepreneurial activity in the material world relatively unimportant and meaningless.

The second worldview component—What is the nature of the world?—is equally important. If as in some worldviews the world is tricky, an illusion, then scientific and innovative action in this world is rendered ultimately frustrating and unnecessary. In a perversion of Christian faith, something we might call a "secularized though religionized 'Christian' worldview" (though it is not really Christian), the physical world and the human body are not as important as the immortal soul and the heaven to which we are going. The thoroughgoing secular mindset maintains that the physical world is all we have, and that it is a diminishing resource, though a resource to be exploited. Others see the physical world as something to be worshiped, not developed through stewardship. It is a widely understood truth that much of the scientific and creative innovation that has taken place in recent centuries has been undertaken on the basis of the Jewish and Christian worldview, namely, that the exploration of physical realities and the development of the potential of creation is a worthwhile, indeed even a holy, enterprise, some half-true critiques to the contrary.[25]

---

[25]We refer to the famous article by Lynn Townsend White Jr., "The Historical Roots of Our Ecologic Crisis," *Science* 155, no. 3767 (1967): 1203-7. The article claimed that the biblical injunction to "rule" and "have dominion" led to the ruthless exploitation of nature, and that therefore the Jewish and Christian faiths are responsible for the state of the planet. This is a half-true assertion in that many people of faith have understood their relation to creation as one of domination rather than stewardship, the latter being the true meaning of the Genesis text.

The contrast between the self-narrative of the humanist model and the God narrative of the Christian model is also reflected in the realm of leadership. While the humanist model focuses on advancement of self, the Christian approach as modeled by Christ is based on what has become known as "servant leadership."[26] Jesus stated, "Whoever wants to become great among you must be your servant" (Mk 10:43). Another passage that is clearly at odds with the humanist model is Paul's advice to the church at Philippi: "Do nothing out of selfish ambition or vain conceit. Rather, in humility value others above yourselves, not looking to your own interests but each of you to the interests of the others" (Phil 2:3-4). For an entrepreneur the resulting actions under the Christian model would have a different starting point than the humanist model. The Christian model represents an orientation away from self-centeredness, and a practical outgrowth is the notion of servant leadership. The humanist model, on the other hand, is rooted in a greater self-focus.

2. Transcendent norms. In contrast with the humanist model, which proposes that ethical norms are created by human beings, the second element of the Christian model is a focus on living according to a divinely given ethic.[27] How do we know right and wrong? The secular viewpoint is that we get this from social consensus. Under some systems the codes of social behavior and obligations are written in a detailed way, prescribing every aspect of life. There is limited room for creativity. An individual diligently follows an external code created by human beings. In other systems, largely in the East, behavior is prescribed by social obligation and hierarchical relationships. For example, young people choose occupations based on their parents' expectations, not their own gifts and talents and their personal passions.

In the postmodern Western worldview absolutes are obsolete. Everything is relative. But from the Christian perspective the laws

---

[26]Robert Greenleaf, *Servant Leadership: A Journey into the Nature of Legitimate Power and Greatness* (Ramsey, NJ: Paulist Press, 1977).

[27]We discuss a Christian approach to ethics further in chap. 8 under the subhead "Principle 2: Making Ethical Decisions."

and lifestyle guidelines given by God are not relative. For example, the Old Testament contains the oft-cited Ten Commandments (Ex 20:1-17). While they were provided to the people of Israel at a particular time and place, most Christians adhere to them, as do many so-called secular people who may not be aware of the source of these ethical absolutes. These decrees of God are basic prescriptions for communal relations.

- "You shall have no other gods before me."
- "You shall not make for yourself an image . . ."
- "You shall not misuse the name of the LORD."
- "Remember the Sabbath day by keeping it holy."
- "Honor your father and your mother."
- "You shall not murder."
- "You shall not commit adultery."
- "You shall not steal."
- "You shall not give false testimony."
- "You shall not covet your neighbor's house."

The Ten Commandments have immediate relevance to the world of work and business in particular, as some contemporary ethicists have shown.[28]

Jesus integrates his teaching with the Ten Commandments and does not abolish them. "Do not think that I have come to abolish the Law or the Prophets; I have not come to abolish them but to fulfill them" (Mt 5:17). In the Sermon on the Mount Jesus provides guidance on a range of matters: murder, adultery, divorce, oaths, an eye for an eye, love for enemies, giving to the needy, prayer, fasting, judging others and the like (Mt 5–7). Christ was asked, "What is the greatest commandment?" Jesus replied that the whole of the Old

---

[28]See David W. Gill, *Doing Right: Practicing Ethical Principles* (Downers Grove, IL: InterVarsity Press, 2004). A new book outlines how the Ten Commandments apply to the workplace: John Parmiter, *Ten at Work: Living the Commandments in Your Job* (Nottingham, UK: Inter-Varsity Press, 2011).

Testament law is summarized in these two commandments: to love
the Lord your God with all your heart and might and self, and to love
your neighbor as yourself (Mk 12:28-34). The contrast with the humanist model is obvious: accountability to a transcendent God
versus the individual's process of self-discovery of principles that
further his or her own ends for an individually determined purpose
in life.[29] Behind this, and the true basis of an ethical life for the
Christian, is a personal relationship with a loving and just God who
invites human beings into a covenant relationship and a covenant
community in which we imitate the way God is God in justice, holiness and love.

3. God-given Spirit gifts. The third aspect of the Christian
model is also a worldview issue. What is a human being? According
to a biblical worldview, the material and the human world are real,
not tricky or illusionary. And therefore the exploration and development of matter is meaningful. Matter is important. And the body,
likewise. We are not simply eternal souls imprisoned in an evil and
temporary body, but ensouled bodies or embodied souls.[30] Our
future is bodily and material, as well as spiritual. With an obvious
play on words, Paul in 1 Corinthians 15 says that life in this world is
characterized by our experience of a "soulish" body—a body expressive of emotions and thoughts and influenced by our environment. The actual phrase used is *natural body* (Greek *sōma psy-
chikon*). After the resurrection of the body when Christ comes again,
we will be raised a spiritual (or "Spirit-ual") body (Greek *sōma
pneumatikon*), a body that expresses perfectly life in the Spirit (1
Cor 15:44). In the spiritual body we will perfectly conform to the
image of Christ. So the human vocation is not simply a spiritual one
but a human one.

God has made creatures that are capable of humanizing the earth,
and in the process become more human themselves. That means

---

[29]See, for example, Ken Blanchard and Phil Hodges, *Leadership by the Book: Tools to
Transform Your Workplace* (New York: William Morrow, 1999).
[30]See Hans Walter Wolff, *Anthropology of the Old Testament*, trans. Margaret Kohl
(Philadelphia: Fortress Press, 1981).

that both God and human beings are in charge of the world. They are partners, but not equal partners. Men and women are stewards entrusted with creation but accountable to the Creator. Human activity is expected and critical, but it is not absolute. In the end, and there will be an end, the conclusion of it all is not a technological paradise or a dreary end in a fizzle or a bang, but the glorious second coming of Christ and the renewal of everything (Rev 21:5). This empowers, but does not make absolute, human activity. As individuals we are not extinguished, reincarnated or merely join the spirits of our ancestors. We are resurrected to a grand rendezvous with our Creator and Redeemer in a completely renewed creation where we will enjoy ongoing creativity (Rev 21:24). We will be more human than we ever could be in this life.

If we are simply animals, then instinct governs everything. Anatomy is destiny. If we are divine, we worship ourselves. In new age spirituality we are divine beings evolving into a higher consciousness. If, as in what we've called a "religionized and secularized so-called 'Christian' worldview," we are precious eternal souls in a disposable and evil body, then the only work worth doing is Christian ministry. Forget entrepreneurship and the business of societal enterprise. We are getting as many souls as we can into a lifeboat to save people from this sinking ship, the cosmos. If, as is indicated by the Bible, human beings are Godlike creatures with capacity to make a difference, to be inventive, to be creative, then entrepreneurship is an expression of who we are. Personality will be a factor, as we have shown in considering what actually makes an entrepreneur, but it is deeper than that. It is a way of seeing life and the world. And that comes from a sense of who we are as human beings.

One aspect of this is the idea of talents and gifts. Within the Christian worldview human beings are endowed with unique and varying capacities. These are from God. Also from God are spiritual gifts, really Spirit gifts, also from God, since it is the Holy Spirit working through a human being. Spirit gifts are provided to glorify God and edify others. Perhaps the best starting point for considering Spirit gifts is the oft-quoted 1 Corinthians 12, a passage that focuses on the gifts as given to believers. The apostle Paul shows how believers are bonded in community through gifts: "Just as a body, though one, has many parts, but all its parts form one body, so it is with Christ" (1 Cor 12:12).

Further, Spirit gifts are not just for the church but even for the world.[31] The only person that the Old Testament says was filled with the Holy Spirit is the craftsman Bezalel (Ex 31:1-4). While Scripture seems to distinguish between so-called natural talents and spiritual gifts, the former being permanent and creational and the latter being temporal and situational, Scripture also suggests that the Holy Spirit anoints natural abilities, such as leadership, giving, teaching and administration, with an extra unction of effectiveness (see Rom 12:1-9). This can happen in the workplace as well as ministry in the church.

Superficially, the Christian model and the humanist model have similarities. Each person is endowed with unique abilities. But here the similarity ends. For the Christian talents and gifts are viewed in a communal sense. They are given for loving our neighbor and for loving God. The discovery of gifts is not for self-fulfillment but for advancement of the kingdom of God. They are not only for building up the faith community but also for service in the world. They are not discovered by a process of individualized self-assessment but by group discernment. But there is more by way of contrast.

4. Divine help. The Christian model proposes that we achieve meaning and goals through divine help rather than self-help. The question of who is in charge of the world—a worldview matter—is a complex one. If, as is suggested by some, human beings are absolutely in control with no interference from a divine being, then it is up to us to invent the future, and we do this, as one psychiatrist and social commentator R. D. Laing suggested, by making human beings into magicians! If, on the other hand, only God is absolutely in charge of the world and expresses himself as indomitable will, as is taught in some religious systems and embodied in certain cultures,

---

[31]See Gordon Fee and R. Paul Stevens, "Spiritual Gifts," in *The Complete Book of Everyday Christianity*, ed. Robert Banks and R. Paul Stevens (Downers Grove, IL: InterVarsity Press, 1997), pp. 943-49.

then human action is rendered meaningless. But if, as a Christian worldview proposes, God shares with human beings the oversight of the world and empowers us to be stewards of creation, including people, and even in a limited sense empowers us to create the future within the overarching sovereignty of God, then human initiative (read "entrepreneurial activity") is inspired. It makes sense. That is what the commission to the first human beings means: create, develop, complete, innovate and implement (Gen 1:26-27).

A most basic doctrinal tenet of Christianity is that faith is focused on God through Jesus Christ, not on us. One writer states that a biblical faith is "the radical abandonment of our whole being in grateful trust and love to that God disclosed in the life, death, resurrection of Jesus Christ."[32] A Christian's focus is not on personal or horizontal strength, but rather on strength that comes through God. As stated in Philippians 4:13, "I can do all this through him who gives me strength." There are many verses throughout the Bible that echo these fundamental truths. Isaiah 40:31 proclaims,

> But those who hope in the LORD
> 　　will renew their strength.
> They will soar on wings like eagles;
> 　　they will run and not grow weary,
> 　　they will walk and not be faint.

As Christians serve, Paul cautions that they should not think of themselves "more highly than you ought" (Rom 12:3). A Christian approach is premised on the need for God's help to achieve meaning and goals.

Even though Norman Vincent Peale gave birth to trends that have evolved into the human potential movement, his focus was still on God as the source of strength, and positive thinking was simply a way to tap into that source.[33] *The Power of Positive Thinking* begins

---

[32]Ramanchandra, *Gods That Fail*, pp. 41-42.

[33]Norman Vincent Peale, *The Power of Positive Thinking* (1952), in *Three Complete Books* (New York: Wings Books, 1992). The inclusion of Norman Vincent Peale indicates that we should not always draw too sharp a distinction between the sources of the humanist and Christian models of entrepreneurship. Peale was, of course, the pastor of Marble Collegiate Church in New York City and espoused a Christian approach, yet his

with "Believe in Yourself" and ends with "How to Draw Upon That Higher Power." The preface to his fortieth edition, written in 1992, states that the book "teaches positive thinking, not as a means to fame, riches or power, but as a practical application of Christianity to overcome defeat and accomplish worthwhile creative values in life."[34] The very allegiance to Christ is a denial of self and the power of self to achieve one's own purposes unaided. It is a partnership.

We highlighted subtle and nuanced differences between the humanist model and the Christian model. But we must now ask, so what?

The Positive Inspiration of a Thoroughly Biblical Worldview

Here is how the biblical worldview—and here we wish to include Jewish as well as Christian mindsets—is not only redemptive but an empowering vision that inspires creative activity. God, the infinite, personal and transcendent being, is the ultimate reality. God has made human beings in his image to be relational and to work: to develop the potential of creation. That involves envisioning, innovating and implementing. Change is essential to entrepreneurship. Change is implicit in five biblical doctrines. First, creation is unfolding and continuing (not finished). Second, human beings are stewards (therefore bringing change). Third, the will of God is not inexorable but an empowering vision (which means we can and should bring change). Fourth, human beings have limited free will (which means change is possible). Fifth, eschatology (last things) proposes that God originally had in mind the wedding supper of the Lamb (Rev 19:7) and invites us to work toward this grand rendezvous, the consummation of the kingdom of God and the transfiguration of heaven and earth (which means that our changes made in this life may become an investment in heaven).

In contrast, according to one worldview, history is not going anywhere. It is cyclical. Another worldview sees the conquering of the

---

writings fed perfectly into the human potential movement, which was secularized and diverted from Peale's Christian underpinnings. As a result Peale contributed to the intellectual underpinnings of both humanist and secular models of entrepreneurship.
[34]Ibid., p. 12.

world by one religion as the ultimate future of everything. The totally secular worldview sees linear cause-and-effect as the dominating model of the future, but the future is not really going anywhere. The biblical worldview is that while there are ups and downs in history, perhaps even a spiral, there is a destination and consummation in the final rendezvous of God, creation and humankind. The question of what happens when we die is related to this.

Do we simply get recycled into the soil or into some other living form, depending on what we have done in this life? In due course we will explore the truth that work in this life and we ourselves have a glorious future—not recycling but resurrection. And the resurrection of the person—the crux of the Christian hope—is not the mere survival of the soul in "heaven" but the renewal of the entire person, along with all created reality, in a new heaven *and new earth* (Rev 21:1, 5). And there is reason to hope that some of our work will more than survive and find its place in the new heaven and new earth, as Paul once said, "your labor in the Lord is not in vain" (1 Cor 15:58). More on this later.

As will be shown, it is not surprising that the Christian and Jewish view of reality has inspired amazing innovation. So what does a biblical worldview mean to entrepreneurial activity?

First, work in this world is meaningful and has both intrinsic and extrinsic value—it participates in God's ongoing work and fulfills the divinely given commission of unpacking the potential of creation.

Second, dualism is displaced by full integration. "Spiritual work" (such as that of a pastor or missionary) is not more holy or acceptable to God than homemaking, business, law and trades. Both are doing "the Lord's work."

Third, the virtues and values that inform our work are the Spirit fruit (roughly parallel to the classic virtues) and the values of the kingdom—care for the poor, integrity, compassion, neighbor love, practical almsgiving.

Fourth, we are motivated from within by a God connection through the Spirit, rather than solely through external pressures and codes, whether written or embodied in social expectations. We have a law given from outside, the Ten Commandments and the law of love, but we also have the law written on our hearts (Jer 31:33-34). God says, "I will put my Spirit in you and move you to follow my decrees and be careful to keep my laws" (Ezek 36:27).

Finally, a biblical worldview suggests that work undertaken with faith, hope and love will last, and purged of sin will find its place in the new heaven and new earth. If that does not inspire creative activity in the world, then nothing else can!

With the clarity of the foundational differences between the humanist and Christian models of entrepreneurship, we now examine some of the core elements of a biblical approach, starting with the soul and spirituality.

For Reflection and Discussion

1. Which aspects of the humanist model have been manifested in your organization, business, church or community? Where do you think this comes from? Do the people you work with recognize the implications of this viewpoint? Why?

2. Which tenets of the Christian model are actually being taught and modeled in your church or Christian group? What can you do to assist the leaders of the church in empowering people for an entrepreneurship that is based on the biblical narrative? What resistances do you think will have to be overcome?

3. What worldview was dominant in your family as you grew up? Name the specific dimensions of this. How has this affected your own approach to work and leisure?

Mini Bible Study. Return to the foundational passage in Genesis 1:1–2:3. If you were creating a worldview only on the basis of this Scripture, what would be the essential elements?

4

Soul and Spirituality

*I'm prepared to contend that the primary location
for spiritual formation is the workplace.*

EUGENE PETERSON,
CHRIST PLAYS IN TEN THOUSAND PLACES

Henry Ford, the founder of the eponymous car maker, was reputed to have said one hundred years ago, separating task and being, "Why is it that I always get the whole person when what I really want is just a pair of hands?" As we will see, that attitude has changed in our present era. *Soul* is a common word in business literature and is used in numerous seminars encouraging people to ramp up their motivation. Chapter three described the humanist and Christian models of entrepreneurship, in other words without or with God. This chapter explores some of the dynamics of the source of entrepreneurship—God. The title of this chapter is admittedly ambiguous, partly because many people today are talking about "spirituality," "soul" and "God," but do not associate this with the Christian faith or any other religion that proposes relationship with a transcendent God. And even if they believe in God, they do not associate this with a traditional religion. Stephen King, the prolific author, reflects a common view when he states, "While I believe in God I have no use for organized religion."[1] Religion is "out," at least in much of the Western world, while soul is "in," even in business schools.

---

[1]Stephen King, *On Writing: A Memoir of the Craft* (New York: Simon & Schuster, 2000), p. 52.

One work describes soul this way: "Our soul embodies our personal philosophy—our sense of meaning, our values, our ethical principles, and our sense of social responsibility."[2] Further, another source defines the soul as "the deepest essence of what it means to be human. The soul is that which ties together and integrates all of the separate and various parts of a person; it is the base material, the underlying platform that makes a person a human being."[3] Despite ambiguity, we must examine the soul further. We must because we go to work as whole persons, as Henry Ford reluctantly confessed, and it is vital to know what this means to our soul.

In this chapter we will begin by noting the extensive recovery of soul and spirituality in the marketplace. We will then examine what the soul is biblically, an important study in view of the confusion even among people of faith. Next we will ask what it means to take your soul to work. Finally, we will consider patterns of spirituality, sometimes called "spiritual disciplines," that are appropriate for people in the marketplace. Such patterns of responsiveness and expressiveness are critical for more than surviving the pressures of work, especially for the entrepreneur.

The Recovery of Soul and Spirituality in the Workplace

One major study of spirituality in the workplace, *A Spiritual Audit of Corporate America*, was conducted by Ian Mitroff and Elizabeth Denton.[4] Respondents to their survey viewed spirituality as "the basic desire to find ultimate meaning and purpose in one's life and to live an integrated life."[5] Their research indicates that in contrast to conventional religion, spirituality is not formal; spirituality is not denominational; spirituality is broadly inclusive; spirituality is universal and timeless; spirituality is the ultimate source and provider of meaning

---

[2]Thomas H. Naylor, William H. Willimon and Rolf V. Osterberg, *The Search for Meaning in the Workplace* (Nashville: Abingdon, 1996), p. 208.

[3]Ian I. Mitroff and Elisabeth A. Denton, *A Spiritual Audit of Corporate America: A Hard Look at Spirituality, Religion and Values in the Workplace* (San Francisco: Jossey-Bass, 1999), p. 5.

[4]For a good overview of spirituality and religion by a highly respected philosopher see Charles Taylor, *A Secular Age* (Cambridge, MA: Belknap Press, 2007), pp. 505-35.

[5]Mitroff and Denton, *A Spiritual Audit of Corporate America*, p. xv.

and purpose in our lives; spirituality expresses the awe we feel in the presence of the transcendent; spirituality is the sacredness of everything, including the ordinariness of everyday life; spirituality is the deep feeling of the interconnectedness of everything; spirituality is integrally connected to inner peace and calm; spirituality provides one with an inexhaustible source of faith and willpower; and spirituality and faith are inseparable.[6] Obviously spirituality has many dimensions. In the context of workplace, these authors view spirituality as a pursuit of meaning in life through an eclectic and personalized endeavor, without need for institutionalized infrastructure. Regardless of its definition, one thing is certain: spirituality is a hot topic today, especially in the workplace. And here is the reason.

Mitroff and Denton observed that "people do not want to compartmentalize or fragment their lives."[7] Rather, people want to have their spiritual side (or soul) acknowledged wherever they go. People discriminate between religion, which is generally bad, and spirituality, which is generally good. They note that

> Religion is largely viewed as formal and organized. It is also viewed as dogmatic, intolerant, and dividing people more than bringing them together. In contrast, spirituality is largely viewed as informal and personal, that is, pertaining mainly to individuals. It is also viewed as universal, nondenominational, broadly inclusive, and tolerant, and as the basic feeling of being connected with one's complete self, others and the entire universe.[8]

There are some implications of this surge of interest often epitomized in what we have called the humanist model of entrepreneurship.

First, people "are hungry for models of practicing spirituality in the workplace without offending their coworkers or causing acrimony."[9] Second, some people, not wanting to use the religiously charged word *soul*, use a more neutral word such as *values*, since *values* carries less emotional baggage, is more acceptable and less

---

[6]Ibid., pp. 23-25.
[7]Ibid., p. xv.
[8]Ibid., p. xvi.
[9]Ibid.

threatening.[10] Last, Mitroff and Denton note that, "We believe that the workplace is one of the most important settings in which people come together daily to accomplish what they cannot do on their own, that is, to realize their full potential as human beings."[11] In due course we will agree with this last statement as we expound the Christian model and understand spirituality biblically. Most of what we encounter in this generalized view operates without any relationship with a transcendent God. The contrast with Christian spirituality, while not absolute, is significant.

One of the best definitions of Christian spirituality or "soul life" comes from the South American theologian Segundo Galilea.

> All spirituality springs from this fundamental fact of a God who loved us first. . . . If Christian spirituality is, before all else, an initiative by and a gift from God who loved us and seeks us, spirituality is then our recognition and response, with all that entails, to this love of God that desires to humanize and sanctify us. This path of spirituality is a process, concrete but never finished, by which we identify ourselves with God's plan for creation. Because this plan is essentially the Kingdom of God and its justice (holiness), spirituality is identification with the will of God for bringing this Kingdom to us and others.[12]

Note the significant dimensions of Christian spirituality. First, it starts with the initiative of a loving God who is seeking relationship with his creatures. Second, spirituality then is not our attempt to ascend to God by spiritual practices or to discover our own internal divinity, but takes the form of "recognition and response." Third, the result of this responsiveness to the seeking God is not that we become angels or religious persons, but more fully human (note our agreement with the humanist emphasis on becoming fully human). Fourth, spirituality then is not a once-for-all event but a continuous process that is concrete but never finished. Fifth, the practical outworking of this spirituality is that we align ourselves with God's intention for his creation,

---

[10]Ibid.
[11]Ibid., p. 7.
[12]Segundo Galilea, *The Way of Living Faith: A Spirituality of Liberation* (San Francisco: Harper & Row, 1988), p. 20.

which is the kingdom or pervasive and life-bringing rule of God on earth. Creating wealth and bringing well-being to people is part of this, as we will see. Finally, this spirituality is not cultivating extraordinary experiences but rather the infiltration of ordinary life with kingdom justice and holiness. With this definition in mind we can now consider the complicated question of the human soul.

The Soul Understood Biblically

In everyday conversation the word *soul* can mean at least two things: (1) a precious human person—as in "Two hundred souls were lost in the plane crash" (note how this use of *souls* is found in the shipwreck story of Acts 27:37 in the older King James Version),[13] and (2) the eternal or immortal part of a human being, an incorruptible core—as in "We commit the body to the grave knowing that she still lives in her soul" (at a graveside). We will see that the first is actually closer to biblical truth than the second. In the Bible *soul* and *spirit* are sometimes used interchangeably to speak of the interior of persons, especially in their longings for relationship with God. To gain a proper view of the soul we must consider both the Old and New Testaments.

1. Soul words in the Old Testament. More often than not *soul* in the Old Testament does not refer to the spiritual/emotional part of a person that can be disconnected from bodily life. *Soul* refers to the person as a longing person.[14] Sometimes *soul* is used for the throat, through which the breath of life passes, showing that the word in Old Testament usage does not mean the spiritual part of a person but rather a person with all kinds of longings—sensual and more-than-sensual. So the soul is often frightened, despairing, weak, despondent, disquieted and even bitter. It can also be satisfied, happy and at rest with God and itself.

As the organ of vital needs, the soul must be satisfied for a person to go on living. Satan, in the duel with God, must spare Job's *nepeš* (the Hebrew word), which simply means his life (Job 2:6). Life, for

---

[13]The TNIV simply says, "Altogether there were 276 of us on board."
[14]Hans Walter Wolff, *Anthropology of the Old Testament*, trans. M. Kohl (Philadelphia: Fortress Press, 1981), p. 10.

biblical persons, is total and cannot be segmented into two parts: a disposable and normally evil shell (the body), and an indestructible spirit core (the soul). Thus the familiar psalm "Praise the LORD, my soul; all my inmost being, praise his holy name" (Ps 103:1) may be simply and helpfully translated "Praise the LORD, with my whole life!" The soul is not a spiritual organ in the human body given at creation or with the renewal of conversion. To touch the soul is to touch the person. It is impossible to have a fully biblical view of human personhood without taking this Old Testament perspective seriously.[15] This is especially important because the church has historically been influenced by Greek philosophy in dividing the person into compartments, the outer evil shell and the inner immortal soul. A lot of devotional literature takes this heretical view.

2. *Soul words in the New Testament.* The New Testament assumed the Old and maintained the inspired view of the essential unity of the human person. Most significant of all, the New Testament hope is not for the immortality of the soul—an essentially Greek concept that involves disparaging the body as a useless encumbrance to the life of the spirit. Instead, the great hope in Christ after death is the resurrection of the body—full personal and expressive life in a new heaven and a new earth. Tragically, some Christian theology has relegated the body to the domain of this world. The body then is something intrinsically sinful, a prison for the soul. This has implications for daily work in this world, namely, that it is not considered very valuable, especially work that does something for other people's bodies. At the same time it is assumed that faith concerns the spirit, which is not of this world. Viewed this way, salvation and spirituality are escapes from bodily life. This diminishes such ordinary things as eating, working and sleeping. And most relevant for our purposes, it diminishes entrepreneurial activity and enterprises in this world. The spiritual person is thus one who abandons sexual expression and lives the celibate life or spends his or her life in spiritual ministry. In contrast, the problem of humankind,

---

[15]Some of this study on "soul" is drawn from R. Paul Stevens, "Soul," in *The Complete Book of Everyday Christianity*, ed. Robert Banks and R. Paul Stevens (Downers Grove, IL: InterVarsity Press, 1997), pp. 922-26.

according to the Bible, lies not in the body (*sōma*) but in the will. What we need is not to get rid of our bodies but to get a new heart (Ezek 11:19).

When we receive Christ, *we* get saved, not just our souls in the Greek sense. This is a two-stage process. First, our souls, our inner and longing persons, are substantially saved by being inundated by God's Spirit, thus giving us new bodily and personal life on earth. Second, after our death and when Christ comes again, we are given a new and perfect embodiment through the resurrection of our entire selves, bodies included. Two stages, but it starts with the substantial transformation of the person.

Our passions do not come from the physical body (perceived as the source of sin) while ideas and moral convictions come from the soul (perceived as the center and source of righteousness). The body is not the prison house of the soul and its seducer into sin.[16] The soul is the seat of life, as indicated in the words of Jesus, "For whoever wants to save their life [soul] will lose it, but whoever loses their life for me and for the gospel will save it" (Mk 8:35).

A related word in the New Testament is *spirit*. Here again there is harmony with Old Testament thought. *Spirit* is that capacity in human beings that relates them to a realm of reality beyond ordinary observation and human control.[17] God encounters people immediately through the spirit (Rom 8:16; 2 Tim 4:22). But it is, once again, a dimension of the whole person. So the popular debate as to whether human nature is two parts (soul and body) or three (spirit, soul and body), the latter based largely on one text (1 Thess 5:23), is unhelpful, a recent major scholarly work on the subject notwithstanding.[18] "The human person is a 'soul' by virtue of being a 'body' made alive by the 'breath' (or Spirit) of God."[19] The spirit is not one compartment of the

---

[16]G. Harder, "Soul," in *New International Dictionary of New Testament Theology,* ed. Colin Brown (Grand Rapids: Zondervan, 1979), 3:682; J. Dunn, "Spirit/Holy Spirit," in *New International Dictionary of New Testament Theology,* 3:692.

[17]Dunn, "Spirit/Holy Spirit," p. 693.

[18]J. W. Cooper, *Body, Soul & Life Everlasting: Biblical Anthropology and the Monism-Dualism Debate* (Grand Rapids: Eerdmans, 1989).

[19]J. E. Colwell, "Anthropology," in *New Dictionary of Theology,* ed. S. B. Ferguson and D. F. Wright (Downers Grove, IL: InterVarsity Press, 1988), p. 29.

Christian person—one boxcar in a three-car train (spirit-soul-body) in which each car could be uncoupled. The spirit is simply one dimension of personhood in a totally integrated personhood that is expressed in bodily activity, emotional life and intellectual thought (soul). Far from being three separate compartments, the human person is a psycho-pneuma-somatic unity. In biblical anthropology we do not *have* a body or soul or spirit; we *are* a body, a soul, a spirit. So what does this mean for entrepreneurial leadership?

Soul Entrepreneurship

First, it means that you go to work as a whole person—not just mind or body, but all that inner yearning and expressiveness that links us with God. We gain this perspective from the God narrative in the Bible. What Henry Ford lamented is indeed a great gift with enlarged resources for entrepreneurial activity.

Second, as soul persons with capacity to relate to God, we are given ideas, visions and perspectives that can be implemented through entrepreneurial activity. These may be in the area of church life but also in family life and enterprises in the world. An example is Nehemiah in the Old Testament, who had the difficult job of rebuilding the wall of Jerusalem and rebuilding the people. He said, "My God put it into my heart to . . ." (Neh 7:5). Bright ideas come from God.

Third, our actual experiences in envisioning, inventing and implementing as entrepreneurs are an arena of spiritual growth. In *Taking Your Soul to Work*, Alvin Ung and I (Paul) argue that we are hardwired by God for God and for Godlikeness.[20] The workplace presents most people with the greatest opportunity for spiritual growth. It is not only where we experience soul-sapping struggles, but it is also where the fruit of God's Spirit gets unfolded within us. This critical spiritual growth does not take place only or even mainly in retreats and church services, but in the rough and tumble of enterprise.

Fourth, being a soul person (and a whole person) means being relationally alive through love. We are most godlike in relationships.

---

[20]R. Paul Stevens and Alvin Ung, *Taking Your Soul to Work: Overcoming the Nine Deadly Sins of the Workplace* (Grand Rapids: Eerdmans, 2010), pp. 1-9.

Persons are not the same as individuals. We are persons not in our individual life but in relationship to God and other people. We were created male and female in the image of the triune God (Gen 1:27)—built by love, in love and for love, called into existence by a personal God who *is* love within a triune community (1 Jn 4:16). So that which most links us with the living God—the soul—links us with our neighbor and with the Christian community. And business is actually a practical way of loving our neighbor, whether that neighbor is near or far, visible or not visible. Business is not only one of the best hopes of the poor of the world, but it is also a way of building community both locally and globally.

Finally, Christian spirituality and its recognition of a soul dimension to human life and work means that personal growth is not a human achievement (through disciplines and practices) but a response to the Spirit's initiative. *Soul* and *spirit*, as we have seen, refer to ways that people can be alive to God. It is a great mistake to consider Christian spirituality as the cultivation of our inbuilt desire for transcendence. Christian spirituality is essentially Spirit-uality—God's empowering presence calling human beings into dynamic relation and expressiveness. Many of the occasions in which *spirit* and *spiritual* are used in the New Testament should be capitalized (*Spirit* and *Spiritual*), though few translations indicate this. Spiritual growth is Spirit growth. Spiritual gifts are gifts of the Spirit. Spiritual life is walking in the Spirit. God makes us fully alive as bodily persons, fully alive together and fully alive forever.

It is appropriate in the light of all this that we now consider patterns of responsiveness to the seeking God, patterns that support the spiritual process before and after we work and patterns within the work experience itself.

Spiritual Disciplines for More Than Surviving

So far we have seen that with regard to "taking your soul to work" you cannot avoid doing it. You go to work as whole persons. And while some have thought that marketplace spirituality is an oxymoron, it really makes wonderful sense, more than sense; it helps us thrive. In chapters eight and nine we discuss in detail the principles behind practicing and sustaining entrepreneurial leadership in the marketplace; for now we are providing some underpinnings in relation to our general discussion of the soul and spirituality. Eugene Peterson says in this chapter's epigraph that he is prepared to admit that the workplace is the primary place for spiritual formation. And how can this be?

1. The marketplace as a location for spiritual formation. The marketplace is a location for spiritual formation in three ways. First, it is the place where we get revealed as persons. Our inside is revealed by what we do outside, by the way we work, by our relationships with people, by the realities of how we go about doing day to day enterprise. Cardinal Wyszynski said that our souls are revealed by the sweat of our brows.[21]

Second, the seven deadly sins, seven soul-sapping struggles that include pride, greed, lust, anger, envy, sloth and gluttony, are revealed not in quiet times and prayer retreats but in the thick of life, in business meetings, as we struggle over this month's sales, when we have to deal with an awkward customer or employee. And every soul-sapping struggle becomes an opportunity to grow spiritually. That is the heart of the book *Taking Your Soul to Work* that Alvin Ung and I (Paul) authored. The fathers and mothers of the church have always said that we cannot know God without knowing ourselves, but they did not mean, as is commonly thought today, knowing our potential, knowing our giftedness and realizing our full potential. They meant knowing how needy we are. Every need becomes a pathway for growth. And the growth that takes place at the point of our struggle is usually one or other dimension of the ninefold fruit of the Spirit: love, joy, peace, patience, kindness, goodness, faithfulness, gentleness and self-control (Gal 5:22-23). But there is a third reason why the workplace is an arena for spiritual growth.

The work that we do, if it is good work, is some part of God's own work in creating, sustaining, transforming or consummating

---

[21]Cardinal Stefan Wyszynski, *All You Who Labor: Work and the Sanctification of Daily Life* (Manchester, NH: Sophia Press, 1995), p. 113.

(bringing things to a good conclusion). We are actually partners with God in our daily work. Paul said to the Colossian slaves that they were actually servants of Jesus, full-time ministers of Jesus (Col 3:24). This brings a transformative dimension to our daily work. It means that instead of regarding work in the world as a diversion from the spiritual life and from the "work of the Lord" (which is normally associated with pastors, missionaries and voluntary work in the church) we are doing "the Lord's work" in creating new products and services, developing the organizational culture of our business, engaging in trading and global enrichment, creating new wealth and improving human life. So how do we go about maximizing the workplace for spiritual growth and so become "more than survivors"?

2. Disciplines of responsiveness and recognition. The workplace is an avenue to practice the disciplines of responsiveness and recognition. What do we mean by this? First, we must practice the "mixed life." That is a phrase that comes from the biblical story of Mary and Martha in Luke 10. A superficial reading of the story puts Mary on the top of the heap as the one who listens to Jesus and gets his approval, with Martha busy in the kitchen and being criticized for fussing about making a gourmet meal for Jesus and his friends. But the story is better understood this way: Martha's actions were not wrong in providing a meal, but her attitude was wrong. She was so anxious to produce a supermeal for Jesus that she didn't even bother to commune with her most important guest, Jesus. And that, Jesus says, is even more important than making a fine meal. Martha was anxious about many things. She tried to triangle Jesus into getting help ("Tell her to help me") and felt unsupported and overworked. We can all identify with that. But the point is not that Martha should become Mary. Rather, Martha and Mary should be doing the same thing: working but communing with Jesus.

That has led people throughout church history to say we need to embody both Mary and Martha in the same person, sometimes at different times. Sometimes we will be busy at work (in the kitchen), but at other times we withdraw from these pressures to attend to God wholeheartedly. A businessman wrote to the monk Walter Hilton in the twelfth century and said he thought he should leave business and go into the monastery. Read the modern translation of this: Leave your business and go into pastoral or missionary work, or serve on a not-for-profit Christian enterprise in the "second half" of your life, finding significance now that you have found success in the first half. This seems like "God has a wonderful plan for the second half of your life." But Walter Hilton responded in his "Letter to a Layman" that he should go deep, not leaving his business but combining business and reflection.[22] That is what Jesus did. He engaged and he withdrew. Do we withdraw? And, if so, what do we do when we withdraw?

Perhaps we are withdrawing for twenty minutes at the beginning of each day, and one full day of sabbath rest and reflection each week, and an occasional two- or three-day retreat in a monastery, retreat center or resort. We read the Bible, ideally reading a chapter from the Old Testament, a Psalm and a chapter from the New Testament each day. This means we read through the New Testament and Psalms twice a year, and the Old Testament in more than year. We can go for a prayer walk in the early morning, tuning out the world and not plugging in ear buds for our iPhone. Many people find journal writing (a kind of written prayer) and prayer with a spouse or friend helpful when they are functioning like Mary. Then they go to work and do Martha's job.[23] But there is more.

Spirituality in the marketplace is not just living a disciplined life of engagement and withdrawal. The warp and woof of everyday business becomes an arena of growth. The workplace is where we get revealed, our strengths and weaknesses, our dysfunctionalities, the soul-sapping struggles that emerge day and night as we undertake to get an enterprise going and growing. And every one of those areas of struggle becomes a nonverbal cry and a prayer to God to please reveal in us some aspect of the fruit of the Spirit (Gal 5). This is especially true of

---

[22]Walter Hilton, *Toward a Perfect Love*, trans. David L. Jeffrey (Portland, OR: Multnomah Press, 1985), p. 8.
[23]This is developed more fully in R. Paul Stevens, *Doing God's Business: Meaning and Motivation for the Marketplace* (Grand Rapids: Eerdmans, 2006), pp. 125-42.

the so-called Achilles' heel, our point of vulnerability, which shows up not in prayer meetings and church services but in day-to-day business. For most of us the point of vulnerability is one of three things: the need to be needed, the need for status or the need to be in control. Sometimes an accountability group, a prayer group of people in the marketplace, a spiritual director or a friend can help us deal with these. In *Doing God's Business*, I (Paul) tell the story of how my supervisor, Walter Wright, said that the job I had just taken on as academic dean of Regent College required me to "deal with myself." And Wright said, "I will help you." Which he did.

So the pressures we face in daily work become an arena for knowing God and growing spiritually. This is especially true as we approach all kinds of tasks and challenges in prayer, the way Brother Lawrence did in *The Practice of the Presence of God:* "Lord, I cannot do this unless you enable me." Business people have as much opportunity and need to pray as do pastors, monks and nuns. You could ask, why pray when God knows what you need even before you ask? That is a question posed by young and old, time and again. And a good answer is: What if God knows that what you need more than anything is God, and what if your asking for things and asking for help is his way of giving you himself? This is especially true with the big challenges we face.

For Reflection and Discussion

1. What comes to your mind when you hear the phrase "taking your soul to work"?

2. Since spirituality is big business today, we cannot avoid relating to the phenomenon. How can you see yourself relating to this emphasis when it is spoken of by others or offered in business seminars in a humanistic way? What points of contact can you confirm? How can you speak of the Christian approach in an inclusive and constructive way?

3. Imagine for a moment that you could be independently wealthy and would never have to work again. Would that be good for your spirituality?

4. What patterns of spiritual nurture have you found helpful in the past? And what disciplines might you consider for the future?

Mini Bible Study. Study the "works of the flesh" and the "fruit of the Spirit" in Galatians 5:19-25. Translate each of the "works" into realities you have encountered in the workplace or in yourself. Consider each dimension of the Spirit's fruit in us as it is a response to and liberation from these soul-sapping struggles.

5

Meaning and Work Ethic

Man's search for meaning is the primary
motivation in his life and not a "secondary
rationalization" of instinctual drives.

VIKTOR E. FRANKL,
MAN'S SEARCH FOR MEANING

Viktor E. Frankl was an internationally known psychiatrist who endured the well-documented horrors of Nazi concentration camps. His World War II experiences, laced with degradation and suffering, shaped his revolutionary approach to psychiatry, which he termed "logotherapy." The heart of his theory was that humankind's primary motivational force is a search for meaning, which is not only an overarching view of life but also an approach with practical consequences. Frankl explains that "the meaning of life differs from man to man, from day to day and hour to hour. What matters, therefore, is not the meaning of life in general but rather the specific meaning of a person's life at a given moment."[1] As Frankl insightfully observed, people are motivated by a pursuit of meaning.

On the same theme, a recent bestselling book counsels readers that "When you are living on purpose you feel that you are making a difference," and "When serving a purpose larger than yourself, your level of commitment also expands."[2] This is something that came

---

1Viktor E. Frankl, *Man's Search for Meaning* (New York: Pocket Books, 1959), pp. 130-31.

2Jack Canfield, Mark Hansen and Les Hewitt, *The Power of Focus* (Deerfield Beach, FL: Health Communications, 2000), p. 278. An interview with Les Hewitt, one of the coau-

out in research among Entrepreneurial Leaders. They were asked to respond to (on a scale of strongly disagree [1] to strongly agree [10]): "I find meaning in my work because I believe God wants me to be doing what I am doing."[3] An overwhelming 60 percent of respondents answered 10.[4] Most considered that their activities in the marketplace were infused with meaning. Admittedly, it may be harder for some people to find deep meaning at work if they are engaged in, for example, laborer positions, some managerial roles or temporary positions. The entrepreneur, in contrast, allows for the self-creation of a job in which he or she can specifically use gifts and talents. Entrepreneurship is often a creative expression of the soul of the person, who is creating something unique that he or she is passionate about and finds meaning in doing. But where does that meaning come from? That is what we will be exploring presently.

In this chapter we will contrast the Christian approach to meaning at work with a secular approach. We will use the humanist and Christian models of entrepreneurship as reference points as we focus specifically on the pursuit of meaning. We will look first at the search for meaningful work in the humanist model, and then consider the theological grounds for meaningful work, or more accurately finding meaning through work rather than in it, a subtle distinction that will be elaborated.

This chapter will contain some theology. Don't be turned off by that term; it is exactly what is needed to make sense of our lives and, in this case, the meaning of our work as entrepreneurs. The Puritan William Perkins once defined theology as "the science of living blessedly forever." It is a science; that is, it involves study. Theological reflection is a way of studying to make sense of something. But that something is not esoteric reality but "living," and in this case the science of working as an entrepreneur. Continuing with Perkins's definition, the subject of our study is not just mere survival

---

thors, is included in *Entrepreneurial Leaders: Reflections on Faith and Work*, ed. Richard J. Goossen (Langley, BC: Trinity Western University, 2007–2010), 4:131-50.
[3]ELQ, section D, question 19, ELRP Analysis.
[4]Ibid.

but living "blessedly," that is, in the light of God's great and life-giving purpose so that individuals fulfill their God-given potential and find meaning in life and work. But first we must deal with the reality and complexity of the search for meaning.

The Humanist Model and Meaning at Work

The most significant challenge of the humanist model to Christian entrepreneurial leaders is that in it the individual looks for meaning in the work itself. In the Christian model the entrepreneurial leader finds meaning in God through and in the context of the work. The humanist approach is exemplified by Michael Gerber, one of the best-read entrepreneurship authors in the marketplace. A measure of his influence is that he has likely outsold all the leading academic authors combined on entrepreneurship.[5] Gerber, in his widely read book *The E-Myth*, asks, "But before you can determine what your role [in your business] will be, you must ask yourself these questions: What do I value most? What kind of life do I want? What do I want my life to look like? Who do I wish to be? Your Primary Aim is your answer to all these questions."[6] The use of the term *primary aim* in this quote is synonymous with the pursuit of meaning in life. The person's business becomes a platform to achieve his or her primary aim, or meaning in life. As Gerber states, "Your Strategic Objective is a very clear statement of what your business has to ultimately do for you to achieve your Primary Aim."[7] Gerber is not alone in voicing this approach.

Richard Leider has written a book on this very topic, *The Power of Purpose: Creating Meaning in Your Life and Work*. Leider chose to write this book based on his "deepened belief that we live in a spiritual world and that every individual in that world has been created in God's image with unique gifts and a purpose to use those gifts to contribute value to that world."[8] Leider explains that "Spirit

---

[5]Gerber's E-Myth series of books have sold well over one million copies. Meanwhile, most textbooks will sell between 5,000-10,000 copies.
[6]Michael Gerber, *The E-Myth: Why Most Small Businesses Don't Work and What to Do About It* (New York: Collins, 1995), p. 135.
[7]Ibid., p. 149.
[8]Richard Leider, *The Power of Purpose: Creating Meaning in Your Life and Work* (San

touches and moves our lives" and that his objective is "not intended to express a religious or denominational belief."[9] We are, rather, again directed to self-discovery. Leider then expands the concept:

> Purpose depends on our intuition. Intuition is that almost imperceptible voice that leads us to our purpose. Intuition is our sixth sense—the sense for the unknowable. It is independent of conscious reasoning. Sometimes we cannot explain how we know something; we just know it. To discover our purpose, we must trust our intuition. The key to acting on purpose is to bring together the needs of the world with our unique gifts in a vocation—a calling. Calling is our way of actively contributing to our world, however we define that world.[10]

Leider expresses concepts that seem compatible with a Christian approach—superficially, yes, but not with any detailed analysis. Leider's approach to calling is rooted in an independent process of discovery rather than anchored in a specific Christian foundation.

Brian Tracy, a well-known self-help guru, echoes this refrain:

> Remember, you were put on this earth to do something wonderful with your life. You have within you, talents and abilities so vast that you could never use them all if you lived to be a thousand. You have natural skills and talents that can enable you to overcome any obstacle and achieve any goal you could ever set for yourself. There are no limits on what you can be, have, or do if you can find your true calling, and then throw your whole heart into doing what you were made to do in an excellent fashion.[11]

Another author states,

> You have a unique purpose for living, and you have been given unique talents and abilities to accomplish that purpose. You need to reflect on your purpose, and discover it, in order to be truly successful. True success always involves personal fulfillment of some kind, and you are fulfilled only by working and living in harmony with your purpose in life.[12]

Francisco: Berrett-Koehler, 1997), p. 3.
[9]Ibid., p. 4.
[10]Ibid., p. 3.
[11]Brian Tracy, *A Treasury of Personal Achievement* (Niles, IL: Nightingale-Conant, 1997), p. 125.
[12]Marc Allen, *Visionary Business: Entrepreneur's Guide to Success* (Novato, CA: New World Library, 1995), p. 29.

In short, the ethos of the humanist model is that the individual finds meaning at work—this is the context in which to reach true fulfillment. The Christian model reflects a critical contrast. We will explore this contrast through the study of biblical characters.

The Old Testament Case Study in Meaningless Work

The Old Testament book of Ecclesiastes is a good starting point for a discussion of meaning and work. The main character in this book, the Professor, poses a question that is probing and not rhetorical: "What do people get for all the toil and anxious striving with which they labor under the sun?" (Eccles 2:22). This question probes the depths of our experience of work. It is asked not only by people at the end of a long hard day at the office or home, and by workaholic professionals and entrepreneurs who have discovered that their exciting careers are mere vanity and emptiness. This we could understand. But it is also secretly asked by people in Christian service careers who wonder if their preaching, counseling and leadership is, in the end, useless and to no avail. "What do people get for all the toil and anxious striving with which they labor under the sun?" Yet it is crucial to observe from the book as a whole that the Professor is not just down on life and in need of counseling. He affirms that "People can do nothing better than to eat and drink and find satisfaction in their toil. This too, I see, is from the hand of God" (Eccles 2:24). So the Professor is in a bind and so are we.[13]

The Professor deepens the bind by telling us why he thinks work is meaningless: First, it is temporary ("under the sun" [Eccles 2:22]). Second, we will eventually be unappreciated ("I must leave them to the one who comes after me" [v. 18]). Third, we may give our best energies and most creative gifts to a job that may be taken over by a fool ("Who knows whether that person will be wise or foolish?" [v. 19]). Fourth, we are certain to experience injustice in the workplace ("For people may labor with wisdom, knowledge and skill, and then

---

[13]Some of these thoughts are found in R. Paul Stevens, *Work Matters: Lessons from Scripture* (Grand Rapids: Eerdmans, 2012).

they must leave all they own to others who have not toiled for it" [v. 21]). Finally, overwork is inevitable ("What do people get for all the toil and anxious striving?" [v. 22]). So work "under the sun" (a code phrase in this book) is impermanent, unappreciated, unproductive, unfair and seductive.

Surprisingly the Professor does not counsel us to cope with this by dropping out or squeezing all the pleasure we can out of life, including our work life. The reason is breathtaking: he is convinced that *it is God's will* for work to be useless! And God speaking through this Professor asks us to reflect on our experience of work because he wants to call us to faith in a God who has determined that work should be useless. There is more revelation and faith in this man's dark ponderings than in many Christian testimonies of getting rich quick and exhortations to praise the Lord on the job.

This question probes our souls deeply. If work, even volunteer work in Christian service, proves to be meaningless, then we are invited to conclude that we were not made for work but for God. If the Professor is right, then we will not find satisfaction in our work through faith in God (the current "Christian" work heresy); instead, we will find satisfaction in our God through our experience of work. It is a subtle but telling distinction. It is the difference faith makes.

So this deep experience of meaninglessness we share with the Professor turns out to be an inspired frustration. His holy doubt gives us the opportunity to find in God what we cannot find in work under the sun. Work is an evangelist to take us to Christ. And the gospel we hear from Jesus is not that if we accept him we will be insanely happy, successful and totally satisfied in our jobs, but that we will find satisfaction in Jesus in our work. He alone can fill the God-shaped vacuum in our souls. So it is not just the Old Testament Professor but Jesus that asks this probing question. With absolute courtesy Jesus comes to us in the workplace not to tell us what to do with our lives but to ask what we are discovering in our search for meaning in our work. And then with infinite grace he offers himself.[14] So where does that leave us in relation to being engaged in entrepreneurial work?

Toward Meaning Through Work

The preposition *through* is important. The Christian approach is not just that we find meaning "in" the work—a good thing, though often incomplete and not fully satisfying—but more exactly, "in the work in relation to God" and therefore "through" it. Fundamentally, people of faith find meaning not simply in the activity, such as entrepreneurial work, but in relation to a transcendent personal God who invites relationship and offers, as Jesus once said, that "My Father will love them, and we will come to them and make our home with them" (Jn 14:23). This is the New Testament way of saying what the Professor concluded as the end of his search for meaningful work, namely that it is through the fear of God (Eccles 12:13)—a relationship of affectionate awe with the living God—that meaning is to be found. There are three facets of this source of meaning.

1. God as the ultimate source of creativity. It all starts with God, who, as Genesis reveals, is a worker. Genesis opens with God at work, the first and finest worker in the universe. David Jenson notes how radical this is:

> One of the distinguishing characteristics of biblical faith is that God does not sit enthroned in heaven removed from work, willing things into existence by divine fiat. Unlike the gods of the Greco-Roman mythologies, who absolve themselves of work [or make work a punishment for troublesome persons, e.g., Sisyphus] dining on nectar and ambrosia in heavenly rest and contemplation—the Biblical God works.[15]

He is imagining, designing, fashioning, speaking into existence, brooding over what he has made and, best of all, enjoying his work. After each creative act God says, "It is good," which is roughly equivalent to saying, "Beautiful! Wow!" There is a significant entrepreneurial dimension of God's activity: envisioning, inventing and im-

---

[14]Some of this reflection from Ecclesiastes is found in ibid.
[15]David H. Jenson, *Responsive Labor: A Theology of Work* (Louisville, KY: Westminster John Knox Press, 2006), p. 22.

plementing. This activity is ongoing. Jesus, speaking centuries later, said, "My Father is always at his work to this very day, and I too am working" (Jn 5:17). One of the most creative things God has made is a rough facsimile of himself—human beings!

The critical chapters in Genesis about the creation of the world and humankind contain a passage that has been the subject of brooding for centuries:

> Then God said, "Let us make human beings in our image, in our
>   likeness." . . .
> So God created human beings in his own image,
>   in the image of God he created them;
>   male and female he created them. (Gen 1:26-27)

Two things distinguish human beings from other animals: First, we are made as relational beings—male and female—in resemblance of the relational God who dwells as a being in communion—Father, Son and Spirit. But the second similarity of human beings and God is the one that occupies us in this book. We are like God in that we are made to work, to invent, to care for creation and to develop the potential of the created order. God is the ultimate wellspring of all human entrepreneurial activity. In what sense may we speak of human work as creative, and co-creativity with God?

2. Human beings' capacity for God-inspired creativity. Several Hebrew words in the Old Testament are used to describe both God's activity and that of human beings. Humankind is not creative in the ultimate sense of creating out of nothing (*bara'*), but in the derivative sense of sharing with God the continuing stewardship and development of the cosmos—cultivating creation (Gen 2:15) and subduing and filling it (Gen 1:28). We "bring the Creator's work to its intended fulfilment by being co-creators in a very grand project," says Michael Novak, the premier Catholic marketplace theologian of the day.[16]

Much work is in one sense a work of the imagination since it requires creating an image in the mind that will later be fleshed out.

---

[16]Michael Novak, *Business as a Calling: Work and the Examined Life* (New York: Free Press, 1996), p. 37.

Entrepreneurs are doing this all the time. First they envision an idea or a process and then they implement it. In a profound sense we are God's imagination (Gen 1:27). God saw us as an image before he painted us on a canvas; he heard us as a song before he sang us into life; he composed us in his mind before he wrote the poem down. So human beings are works of art and are created to be artful. All good work is in one sense art, since it involves linking the inner and outer life. The inner and outer life, however, are not always successfully linked. This linking of the inner life with the outer is notably lacking in the sluggard in the Proverbs:

> The craving of sluggards will be the death of them,
> > because their hands refuse to work.
> All day long they crave for more,
> > but the righteous give without sparing. (Prov 21:25-26)

Derek Kidner says, "The sluggard lives in his world of wishing which is his substitute for working. It can ruin him materially (v. 25) and imprison him spiritually (v. 26), for he can neither command himself nor escape himself."[17]

Human beings are capable of creating new things. As Dorothy Sayers puts it,

> A true work of art, then, is something *new*—it is not primarily the copy or representation of anything. It may involve representation, but that is not what makes it a work of art. It is not manufactured to specification, as an engineer works to a plan—though it may involve compliance with the accepted rules for dramatic presentation.[18]

Entrepreneurs not only create something new but in so doing express something of themselves, for that is the way we are constitutionally constructed. Henry Mintzberg explains that entrepreneurship is "a practice that has to blend a good deal of craft (experience) with a certain amount of art (insight) and some science

---

[17]Derek Kidner, *Proverbs*, Tyndale Old Testament Commentaries (Downers Grove, IL: InterVarsity Press, 1962), p. 145.

[18]Dorothy L. Sayers, *Christian Letters to a Post-Christian World* (Grand Rapids: Eerdmans, 1969), p. 77.

(analysis)."[19] Our human entrepreneurial activities are derived from our entrepreneurial Creator. But the Genesis account says something further that makes the sacred-secular divide, so common in Christians in all countries, a tragic and antiquated perspective.

3. Filling the earth through God-inspired creativity. As workers, human beings are called to extend the sanctuary (the Garden) into the world, to "fill the earth" (Gen 1:28) by not only populating creation with more human beings but filling it with the glory of God by humanizing the earth through creative work. We do this through inventing better cell phones, farming the land, designing improved computer programs, developing educational programs and creating better images. The Bible makes it clear that we are vice-regents over creation and therefore are commanded to act as stewards of God's created world. In some religions where matter is deified, humans do not enjoy the same dignity and cannot exercise the same responsibility. But biblically creation is neither an idol to be worshiped (as with some religious systems and some new age beliefs) nor a curse.

The two words used by God in his command (Gen 2:15) to Adam to describe work are ʿābad (work) and šāmar (take care). Interestingly, these words are also used to mean "service to God" and "keeping of his commandments," respectively. This implies that no distinction between sacred and secular work can be made. Likewise the word *diakonia,* a Greek word found in the New Testament, is used both for the ministry of the word and service at tables in Acts 6:2, 4. New Testament scholar I. Howard Marshall has shown that the idea that the gathering of the early church was mainly for worship is not supported by the record of the early church. "To sum up what goes on in a Christian meeting as being specifically for the purpose of 'worship' is without New Testament precedent. 'Worship' is not an umbrella-term for what goes on when Christians gather together."[20] Commenting on this Robert Banks remarks on how

---

[19]Henry Mintzberg, *Managers, Not MBAs: A Hard Look at the Soft Practice of Managing and Management Development* (San Francisco: Barrett-Koehler, 2004), p. 1.
[20]I. Howard Marshall, "How Far Did the Early Christians Worship God?" *The Churchman* 99, no. 3 (1985): 9.

little the words for worship are used for the corporate gathering of Christians and offers, again textually, how worship of God is mostly related to life and work.

> One of the most puzzling features of Paul's understanding of *ekklēsia* for his contemporaries, whether Jews or Gentiles, must have been his failure to say that a person went to church primarily to "worship." Not once in all his writings does he suggest that this is the case. Indeed it could not be, for he held a view of "worship" that prevented him from doing so. . . . Since all places and times have now become the venue for worship, Paul cannot speak of Christians assembling in church *distinctively* for this purpose. They are already worshipping God, acceptably or unacceptably, in whatever they are doing. While this means that when they are in church they are worshipping as well, it is not worship but something else that marks off their coming together from everything else that they are doing.[21]

For example, Romans 12:1-2 invites us to present our whole bodily life, including work, to God as a living sacrifice and our spiritual worship. So the dualism that pervades most Christian worldviews that some work is secular and other work, such as evangelism and edification, is sacred is heretical. Why?

It is important to note that the command to work was given *before* the fall and hence is meant to be a blessing and not a curse. Sweaty toil and conversely the idolatry of work are the *result* of the fall. The suspicion with which many Christians regard vocations in the marketplace may be because they think such work is often driven by selfish ambition for wealth, power or money, as was the case with the Tower of Babel (Gen 11) and still is present. These same ambitions are as likely to exist in church and nonprofit contexts. In this life all our motives are always mixed, but essentially entrepreneurs are doing holy work, God-honoring work and even worshipful work. As God-imaging creatures they are doing "the work of the Lord." Yes! What a difference that makes!

---

[21]R. Banks, *Paul's Idea of Community: The Early House Churches in their Historical Setting* (Grand Rapids: Eerdmans, 1980), pp. 91-92.

Good Theology as a Foundation for Good Entrepreneurship

A clear understanding of biblical insights regarding the entrepreneurial dimension of God's activity and its relation to human creativity should be an empowering foundation for entrepreneurs in
their daily activity. Just how does a theology of entrepreneurship
bring strength together and especially to an entrepreneurial leader?

First, the entrepreneur should be *motivated* by the example of
God, the example of Jesus and the truth built into the creation about
the human being that we were made for this. And the world was
made for this. Entrepreneurial activity can be pursued as a holy undertaking, a coparticipation in an ongoing God-ordained process,
with challenges and struggles, but ultimately of great value to the
building of God's kingdom. While in mainstream research the
primary source of motivation for entrepreneurship comes from
within a person and then works itself out, for Christians it comes
from the outside—divinely instigated—and then works inside a
person. An overarching motivation for Christian entrepreneurs
should tie into biblical truths. Our Creator God has made people to
reflect his entrepreneurial activity, and humans participate in his
grand plan of transforming everything. But there is another comfort.

Second, the entrepreneur is *persuaded* that some risks are worth
taking and can be reasonably assessed. In chapter six we discuss risk
and reward at length, but for now we simply point out that there will
be no reward without risk, but the risks are to be calculated. In this
way the entrepreneur's risk taking is like the risk of faith. It is not a
leap in the dark, trusting a God who is totally unknown, but at the
same time the risk of faith requires moving even beyond the security
of reason. Søren Kierkegaard compared not taking risks to the
swimmer who keeps his toe on the bottom of the ocean and refuses
to trust the buoyancy of the water. Becoming a child of God, often
described as "becoming a Christian," is not simply an intellectual
exercise leading to a logical conclusion. One has to take one's toe off
the bottom and trust the buoyancy of the love of God.

So if entrepreneurs are persuaded to have faith, they are *com-
forted* to have hope. What we are doing in entrepreneurial work is

investing in heaven, making a mark on heaven. To the existential question of whose work lasts and what work lasts, biblical theology has a wonder-full answer: work done for God in faith, hope and love. Our "labor in the Lord is not in vain" (1 Cor 15:58). All our work in this life will pass through the refining fire, as Paul says (1 Cor 3:12-15), but if done with Christ, for Christ and in Christ, it will pass in some way beyond our imagination and be part of the wedding supper of the Lamb. Some of our books will be there (possibly even this one!), some meals cooked, some lectures given, some furniture made, some conversations, purged in fire as ore is placed in a cauldron and the dross burned out, leaving the pure metal (2 Pet 3:10-13). And in heaven itself, more accurately the new heaven and the new earth, certainly not a fixed, static and boring reality, there will be infinite scope for invention, envisioning and implementing as we rule with Christ for ever and ever (Rev 22:5). So who would not want to be an entrepreneur!

Throughout this chapter we have been contrasting the humanist model with the Christian model, in particular how in the former, meaning is sought in the work itself, and in the latter, meaning is found mainly in relation to the God for whom and with whom one works. This is not to say that the work itself is totally without meaning, but that ultimate meaning in entrepreneurial work, or any other kind of work, will be found in relation to the God who made us for himself, not primarily for work. One way of understanding this more deeply is through the idea of "work ethic," that is, what makes a person work the way he or she does, or why a person works hard (or not).

Toward a Christian Work Ethic

Typically entrepreneurs are highly motivated, and for multiple reasons, including—as has already been mentioned—the self-satisfaction of being captain of one's own ship. But the question of what makes an entrepreneur tick is an important one. The technical term for this is *work ethic*.[22] Work ethic gets at the guts of the matter:

---

[22]This term must be distinguished from workplace ethics, which is how we determine right and wrong actions in the workplace.

Why work? Why work hard? Why do some people not "get into" their work? Why are some fully engaged? Why work well? So in these closing thoughts we will explore the meaning we have in our work in relation to God himself.

The truth that we are working for God is expounded by two Protestant work ethics, the original in Luther—who affirmed that the work of a nun or priest is no more holy and pleasing to God than the common laborers'—and the "Protestant work ethic," popularized by Max Weber.[23] The Orthodox or Eastern Church, as expressed consummately by Alexander Schmemann in *For the Life of the World*, maintains that human beings are priests of creation, priests ministering to God, to creation and to one another.[24] So what does it mean to find meaning in relation to God and working for God? To this question the Bible gives ten rich answers.

First, we work to glorify God. The apostle Paul says that even slaves are actually serving Christ (Eph 6:5-8; Col 3:22-25). Glorifying God does not mean only singing hymns and spiritual songs, and doing explicit Christian work, but bringing honor to our Creator by the way we work and what we actually do. Bringing glory to God is the master concept of the Christian life. Work then becomes worship. In our work we have an opportunity to love God and even tell God that we love God. This is fundamental to our posture before God, as Jesus taught (Mk 12:29-34). As Cardinal Wyszynski said, "If we love God in our work, it is impossible not to tell Him so."[25] J. S. Bach had it right. He wrote over every manuscript what we can write over balance sheets, sermons and shopping lists: "SDG," which means *soli Deo gloria* (to God alone be the glory).

Second, we work to be partners with God. We are mandated in Genesis as part of the human vocation to serve God and God's purposes in unfolding the potential of creation (Gen 1:26-28). The Garden was

---

[23]Max Weber, *The Protestant Ethic and the Spirit of Capitalism*, trans. Talcott Parsons (New York: Charles Scribner's, 1958).
[24]Alexander Schmemann, *For the Life of the World: Sacraments and Orthodoxy* (Crestwood, NY: St Vladimir's Seminary Press, 1988), p. 15.
[25]Stefan Cardinal Wyszynski, *All You Who Labor: Work and the Sanctification of Daily Life,* (Manchester, NH: Sophia Institute Press, 1996), p. 72.

unfinished. We are God's partners in bringing it to conclusion, and we have not yet done that. This is God's intent for everything he has made.[26]

Third, we work to express gifts and talents through our work. And in this we find joy, the joy of making a difference (Gen 2:19). We are also accountable to God for what we do with our gifts and talents (Mt 25:19).

Fourth, we work to provide for ourselves and our families (1 Thess 4:9-12; 2 Thess 3:6-13). If at all possible we are not to be dependent on others for our livelihood.

Fifth, we work as a witness, showing something of God's goodness and grace to those who do not yet have faith (1 Thess 4:9-12). Paul says that through our work we win the respect of outsiders. Work then is part of our mission and a means of evangelism, a concrete sharing of faith.

Sixth, we work to serve our neighbor. Work is a means of loving our fellow human beings through providing goods or services. This is the second great commandment Jesus taught (Mk 12:29-31). As both Luther and Mother Teresa have said, if we are motivated by love, it does not matter whether we do a great work or a little one.

Seventh, we work to assist the poor and needy. The surplus of what we actually need provided through work can be shared with others who are in need (Eph 4:28). This also is love work.

Eighth, we work to advance the kingdom of God. The kingdom of God is both here and coming, now and not yet. But it is the dynamic rule of God in all of life; it is God's shalom for people and creation. Contrary to much so-called Christian teaching, we advance the kingdom not just by evangelism and edification (the kind of work pastors do) but also by providing goods and services to others. That is what entrepreneurs do. All good work is kingdom work.

Ninth, we work to grow spiritually in Christlikeness. Alan Richardson, in his classic *Biblical Doctrine of Work*, says, "The human being is so made that not only can he not satisfy his material needs

---

[26]Significantly this is a major Jewish emphasis in the theology and spirituality of work. See Jeffrey K. Salkin, *Being God's Partner: How to Find the Hidden Links Between Spirituality and Your Work* (Woodstock, VT: Jewish Lights, 1994).

without working but also he cannot satisfy his spiritual needs, or fulfil his function as a human being."[27] Work is an arena of spiritual challenges, where the seven deadly sins are manifested most explicitly. But it is also the place where the Spirit fruit is revealed.[28] When we work, we have an opportunity to observe ourselves, even to deal with ourselves, our Achilles' heel, our need to be needed, our need for status or our need to be in control. Work is an arena for learning patience, for gaining wisdom, even from our mistakes, and for learning how to pray as we are often pushed beyond the limits of our own abilities.

Tenth, we work to experience joy. Joy is more than mere happiness, though it is often confused with it. Happiness is situational. Joy does not depend on the context. Joy is a God infusion, a God exhilaration, and a God gift. Joy is a part of the fruit of the Spirit (Gal 5:22-23). Knowing that joy is fundamental to the very being of God. Nehemiah counseled the Israelites in a difficult situation to find joy in God and be strengthened by that joy (Neh 8:10). God is not a deadpan autocrat or a celestial killjoy. God is the most joyful being in the universe. And those who have a relationship with God are joyful.[29]

There is the joy *of* working. We were made for it. Then there is joy *in* work. Work involves the use of gifts and talents, everything from organizing, envisioning, inventing, implementing, to beautifying, expressing, communicating and evaluating. All talents are from God. They are not "natural." The exercise of these talents brings joy. "God made me fast," said Eric Liddell, the Olympic runner in *Chariots of Fire*, "and when I run I feel God's pleasure." There is joy *through* work. All good work is a means of serving and loving our neighbor, whether the neighbor is near or far, visible or invisible. Then there is the joy of doing God's work. The multifaceted human occupations all are forms of "doing the Lord's work." More still, there is the joy of consciously working for God. And finally there is the joy of knowing

---

[27]Alan Richardson, *The Biblical Doctrine of Work* (London: SCM, 1954), p. 22.
[28]See R. Paul Stevens and Alvin Ung, *Taking Your Soul to Work.*
[29]See Dennis Bakke, *Joy at Work: A Revolutionary Approach to Fun on the Job* (Seattle: PVG, 2005).

that some of our work done in Christ and for God will last into eternity and form part of the new heaven and new earth (1 Cor 3:12-15; 15:58; Rev 21:24, 26). And more joy still, in the renewed creation we will work with greater joy than we have in this life (Is 65:21-22).

For Reflection and Discussion

1. What was the meaning of work in your home as you grew up?

2. What is the work ethic that has dominated the culture of your own country or people group?

3. What is the work ethic that is taught—either overtly or covertly—in your church or religious group?

4. Of the ten reasons for work listed in this chapter, which ones are actually operative in your life, in your business, in your church or in your community?

Mini Bible Study. Read Ephesians 1:15-23 and Ephesians 2:8-10. What does it mean to you that we are God's "handiwork" (2:10)? What does it mean practically to you that we are created "to do good works" (2:10)?

6

Risk and Reward

The capacity to manage risk, and with it the appetite
to take risk and make forward-looking choices,
are key elements of the energy that drives
the economic system forward.

PETER L. BERNSTEIN,
AGAINST THE GODS

One significant element of business in general and entrepreneurship in particular is the balance between risk and reward. Risk is undertaken for a reason—for gain that is determined to be reasonable in light of the possible reward. The word *risk* derives from the early Italian *riscare*, which means "to dare."[1] Entrepreneurs constantly balance and assess daring to innovate with the likelihood of rewards in the event of success. We will first examine risk and then later turn to reward.

Entrepreneurs are at the cutting edge of business or not-for-profits with their pursuit of innovation, typically doing what has not been tried previously and anticipating that they can master the forces of risk. The reality is that many entrepreneurs miscalculate risk and their businesses fail. On the other hand, entrepreneurs that successfully manage risk by judging and anticipating market trends reap commensurate rewards. Money is lost and gained in various sectors, from mineral exploration to high tech and social media. Between the headlines recounting the tales of the winners and losers is the ongoing tale of managing risk. While we admittedly approach

---

[1]Peter L. Bernstein, *Against the Gods: The Remarkable Story of Risk* (New York: John Wiley, 1996), p. 8.

these questions from the perspective of the Christian faith, we believe that people of all faith traditions can profit from the following analysis of risk and reward.

The Risk-Taking Entrepreneur

Without some risk there will be no innovation. But successful entrepreneurs are neither risk averse nor risk addicted. Peter Drucker believes entrepreneurs are not risk-focused but opportunity-focused.[2] They minimize risk rather than maximize it. Drucker argues that innovation is considerably less risky than optimization. "Entrepreneurs, by definition, shift resources from areas of low productivity and yield to areas of higher productivity and yield. Of course, there is risk they may not succeed. But if they are even moderately successful, the returns would be more than adequate to offset whatever risk there might be."[3] Thus, he concludes, "Theoretically, entrepreneurship should be the least risky rather than the most risky course."[4] But without embracing risk the opportunity will be lost. Entrepreneurs have a unique perspective on risk.

Is the approach of Christian entrepreneurs to risk the same as that of non-Christians? There is a theological perspective on risk that is quite helpful but has likely not been considered by most entrepreneurs. How does their instinctive approach to risk reflect their overall understanding of reality, the role of God and the predictability or whim of events?

1. The risk-taking God. The God of the Bible was a risk taker. God may be described in many ways, but rarely as a risk taker. God took a risk in making everything in such a way that there would be growth and development. That is true of inanimate creation and nonhuman living creatures. God's approach to creation is similar to how entrepreneurs approach their craft. Entrepreneurs, as Drucker says, "see change as the norm and as healthy. Usually they do not

---

[2]Peter F. Drucker, *Innovation and Entrepreneurship: Practice and Principles* (New York: Harper & Row, 1985), p. 139.
[3]Ibid., p. 28.
[4]Ibid.

bring about the change themselves. But—and this defines entrepreneur and entrepreneurship—the entrepreneur always searches for change, responds to it, and exploits it as an opportunity."[5]

Genesis tells us that God placed the man and the woman in a garden of opportunity—but God did not determine what they were to do with it.[6] He did not control them. He commissioned them to have dominion, to develop the potential of creation, to fill the earth (Gen 1:26-28), but he did not force them to do it. He placed them in a world where everything was open to change, and he took the risk that they would fail. But at the same time God was prepared, should they make a mess of their human vocation, to somehow redeem them and their mistake to make something even better. Then God placed before the man and the woman the most risky thing of all, both for God and for Adam and Eve—the tree of the knowledge of good and evil (Gen 2:17), explaining that they were not to eat from it. Why this test? We could ask the same question of the much later narrative in the Bible of Jesus in the wilderness, drawn by the Spirit to be tempted by the devil. Why this test of the sinless Son of God?

If there is no test, there is no growth. And Adam and Eve could never become mature and more fully human unless they were faced with this risky possibility. Would they take provision ("good for food"), pleasure ("pleasing to the eye") and power ("desirable for gaining wisdom" [Gen 3:6]) as something seized for itself, living everyday life as practical atheists, or would they see all of life—working, playing, relating—as part of their communion with God? The tree has been often called the autonomy tree. Why did God take this risk? He could have made them automatons and programmed them to do exactly what he wanted. Using Drucker's framework again, we could view God as opportunity focused on the possibility that people would grow up and become fully human. God, that sovereign risk taker, knew he could compensate for the mistakes made by his creatures

---

[5]Ibid., pp. 27-28.
[6]For additional insight on this topic see chap. 3, "Launched in Hope: Creation and Entrepreneurship," in Richard Higginson, *Faith, Hope & the Global Economy* (Nottingham, UK: Inter-Varsity Press, 2012), pp. 43-62.

should Adam and Eve make the wrong choice, which they did. God's response is called redemption and led eventually to the promise to Abraham and God's coming in person in Jesus. It is intriguing to ask whether in risk analysis one should always be able to foresee a way of redemption. Perhaps one could call this a plan B. But one thing is certain. Each individual's worldview, which may fall on the spectrum from a vague notion of a divine entity to a clearly articulated Christian perspective, will help shape an approach to risk. Those with a biblical understanding of God will be affected, even if it is not precisely articulated, in terms of whether they take risks at all and how much, matters critical to all business ventures and human enterprises. Jesus tells a fascinating story of risk and reward rooted in how individuals view God.

Hardly any part of Scripture is more eloquent on the question of risk than the parable of the talents told by Jesus (Mt 25:14-30). It is a parable about the kingdom of God, the dynamic rule of God in the realities of life. Jesus tells the story with a few deft strokes. A master trusts three servants with his wealth—talents were a measure of money or gold—while the master goes away. Each servant gets what the master thinks he is capable of undertaking as a steward: five to one, two to another and one to a third. But there is a surprise ending.

When the master returns, the five has made five more through opportune investment, through taking a risk. The two has made two more. In both cases the master commends the steward and invites them to enter the master's joy. But the one-talent man simply hands it back intact, without investment. The master's response seems out of proportion to the mistake. The one-talent man is soundly condemned as a wicked servant and is cast out. Why? He had not squandered the talent, left it around to be stolen or wasted it. Why such a judgment? Here is the reason: he had a wrong view of stewardship—preservation rather than investment. He also had a wrong view of the kingdom of God—there is nothing to do but sit around and wait for its coming. But supremely the one-talent man had the wrong view of the master. "I knew that you are a hard man, harvesting where you have not sown and gathering where you have not scattered seed. So I was afraid and went out and hid your gold in the ground. See, here is what belongs to you" (vv. 24-25). That one-talent man was risk averse; the other two were careful risk assessors. The one thought of a risk-fearing God; the other two understood a risk-taking God. This is a contrast between a deficient theology based on fear and a vibrant one grounded in boldness.

2. *The Trinity and entrepreneurship.* Such deficient theology is elaborated in two seminal books, neither of which is normally considered theological, though both are profoundly so. In *The Creation of Wealth*, an older classic volume on capitalism, Brian Griffiths develops the influence of the Trinity on wealth creation. The truth that God is both one and three—Father, Son and Spirit—is unique among world religions. It means that God is not alone; instead God is personal and is a being in communion. Griffiths continues to show how the triune God inspires creativity and entrepreneurship.[7] But a second book goes further.

Peter Bernstein shows how the ancient world, as exemplified in Greek dramas, portrayed the helplessness of human beings in the grasp of impersonal fates. The gods were foolish and fickle. As an aside he explores his own tradition of Talmudic reasoning as a first step toward quantifying risk. But as he proceeds to develop the history of risk analysis, Bernstein notes how up to the Renaissance "people perceived the future as little more than a matter of luck or the result of random variations, and most of their decisions were driven by instinct."[8] Bernstein then traces how the Arabs invented the amazing mathematic system that is used everywhere to this day. But why, he asks, did they not use this system to analyze risk (so critical in any entrepreneurial venture)?

The reason he proposes is their view of God or the gods (think "master" in the parable of Jesus)—gods to be feared and to which one must submit inexorably. They are not to be angered or "played with." Then the author traces how, with the spread of Judaism and

---

[7]Brian Griffiths, *The Creation of Wealth: A Christian's Case for Capitalism* (Downers Grove, IL: InterVarsity Press, 1984).
[8]Bernstein, *Against the Gods*, p. 18.

Christianity, the will of a single God became the orienting reality for the future. This was particularly true of the Protestant Reformation, as it replaced the confessional, since it "warned people that henceforth they would have to walk on their own two feet and would have to take responsibility for the consequences of their decision."[9] This opened up the possibility of trade and "the growth of trade transformed the principles of gambling into the creation of wealth," with the inevitable result of the growth of capitalism, which is "the epitome of risk-taking."[10] But let us summarize why good theology—especially our view of God—actually encourages thoughtful and careful risk taking.

3. Thoughtful and careful risk taking. First, our creative God made creative beings that have the capacity to innovate, to explore, to design and to develop creation. Second, the God revealed in Scripture and embodied in Jesus is not "hard," as the one-talent man thought, but able to forgive and even to make good out of the mistakes we make (Rom 8:28). Love rather than fear becomes the motivation. Third, the biblical view of material reality, unlike some views that reality is tricky and unreliable, or the pantheistic view that it is so divine that it should not be touched, means that the exploration and development of creation is meaningful, result-full and to some extent even predicable.[11] That is, risk analysis is possible. But finally—a matter we will take up in chapter seven in the context of calling—the will of God is not ambiguous or inexorable but an empowering vision of greatness that inspires initiative and opportunism.

So it is a sin to squander what God has given us to use, to wrap our talents, our ideas, our dreams in a handkerchief and bury them for fear of losing them through a risky experiment or for fear of doing our work incorrectly. Faith in a personal God, the God revealed by Jesus, keeps us from pursuing pinched lives. Rather we can live and work exuberantly, knowing that we are accountable not for the pres-

---

[9]Ibid., p. 20.
[10]Ibid., pp. 20-21.
[11]L. T. Jeyachandran, "Towards a More Biblical View of Matter," *Vocatio* 6, no. 1 (2002): 1-3.

ervation of everything but their investment, and expecting that the result of such investment will be "a good measure, pressed down, shaken together and running over. . . . For," as Jesus said, "with the measure you use, it will be measured to you" (Lk 6:38).

In many of his parables Jesus presents an apparently ridiculous view of God—though one often held subconsciously—to shock people into converting to the real God, who is not immovable and harsh but wonderfully personal. Though Jesus does not actually say this, he expects us to think, "Believe in a God who will squeeze everything he can out of you, who will never forgive a mistake, who will swat you down to hell if you mess things up even once, and this is what you get: a pinched, unimaginative, no-risk-taking and utterly deadly life. Believe in the God and Father of the Lord Jesus, and you will be inspired to try things out, to experiment, to take risks and to flourish." So instead of squandering or hoarding with such a God, we are invited to *invest*, risky as it is. But what is investment?

One way of considering investment is to focus on the return we receive. But there is another way of considering the matter of investment. God is looking for a return on his investment in us (Mt 25:19). What we do with assets and money entrusted to us is like a foreshadowing of the last judgment. Our use declares what we really think about God. The gambler has no faith in God but hopes for good luck. The hoarder believes in a vengeful, demanding God. The investor declares that God can be trusted, that God gives what is required and that all investments made with faith, hope and love will bear a return, if not in this life then in the next.[12] So where does that leave the entrepreneur? Does this mean a guaranteed success story? No, but the process of seeing an opportunity, innovating and making something happen, and possibly succeeding on that particular occasion leads to the satisfaction of growing closer to God through work.

---

[12]Some of this section on investment is adapted from R. Paul Stevens, "Investment," in *The Complete Book of Everyday Christianity*, ed. Robert Banks and R. Paul Stevens (Downers Grove, IL: InterVarsity Press, 1997), pp. 540-45.

The Reward-Seeking Entrepreneur

We have seen that risk is part of how God has designed both us and creation. God and the Trinity are risk oriented. Likewise, risk is part of the human condition. What about rewards emanating from the risk undertaken that contribute to the success of an individual? How should Christians approach success—is it solely monetary or a well-balanced life, or simply having reached one's own potential? Is financial success a just reward for having fulfilled one's destiny of being a risk taker? We address the dimensions of success from a biblical perspective, bearing in mind the particular challenges of entrepreneurial leaders.

Success is a paradox. Just when we have achieved it, or so we think, we discover that we are truly a failure. The classic tale of King Midas is illustrative of this. He wanted the power to turn everything to gold, and when he got it his daughter turned to gold when he touched her and his food became gold as well. He nearly starved to death. That is the plight of many so-called successful people—starved to death of meaning and relationships. Tragically even some Christian churches have been co-opted into a secular definition of success in the heretical "health and wealth" gospel. "Serve God and get rich." "God wills your prosperity and health."[13] In this chapter we will explore reward, success by another name, as an enigma. We will consider a biblical case study in the person of the Professor. We will ask what the New Testament has to say on the subject. We will then consider the reframing of success proposed by a contemporary author. We will then ask what are the exact temptations experienced on the road to success. And finally we will try to get inside the truly successful person through insights in the New Testament.

1. Rewards in the Old Testament. The classic study on rewards was done centuries ago by a professor (or preacher) whose firsthand research is contained in the Old Testament—the book of Ecclesiastes. The question posed by the Professor in this book is probing and not rhetorical: "What do people get for all the toil and

---

[13]See Gordon D. Fee, *The Disease of the Health and Wealth Gospels* (Costa Mesa, CA: The Word for Today, 1979).

anxious striving with which they labor under the sun?" (Eccles 2:22). The inspired author (probably someone of considerable means that has taken on the persona of King Solomon) himself is genuinely searching for an answer, and not merely exciting interest in the answer he is about to supply.

Qoheleth or Ecclesiastes, the Professor, comes to some surprising conclusions about being successful. Remember that this important person who took on the persona of King Solomon was examining the meaning of life "under the sun," without reference to a personal transcendent God, and then, as a conclusion, considering work in a reverent affectionate relationship with God—the "fear of the Lord." In his experiential research he comes to some invigorating discoveries.

First, he concludes that we are to work not to be useful or to prove our identity, but because it is a gift of God. "People can do nothing better than to eat and drink and find satisfaction in their toil. This too, I see, is from the hand of God, for without him, who can eat or find enjoyment? To the person who pleases him, God gives wisdom, knowledge and happiness" (Eccles 2:24-26). "That each of them may eat and drink, and find satisfaction in all their toil—this is the gift of God" (Eccles 3:13).

Second, there is more to life than material success because it will surely let us down. Material success will be subject to diminishing returns of satisfaction.

> Those who love money never have enough;
>> those who love wealth are never satisfied with their income.
>> This too is meaningless.
> As goods increase,
>> so do those who consume them.
> And what benefit are they to the owners
>> except to feast their eyes on them?
> The sleep of laborers is sweet, . . .
> but the abundance of the rich
>> permits them no sleep. (Eccles 5:10-12)

Third, we are to "get into" life even though all our projects and even our bodies are doomed to the grave. "Whatever your hand finds to do, do it with all your might, for in the realm of the dead, where you are going, there is neither working nor planning nor knowledge nor wisdom" (Eccles 9:10).

Fourth, we are to take the risk of investing and not wait around for the perfect situation. The image Qoheleth uses is derived from the grain trade of the ancient world. A grain merchant in Egypt needs to send the grain to Italy by ship but there is a cloud in the sky. There is the possibility of a storm. Or the farmer could hold back sowing seed because there is a wind that might lead to a storm.

> Ship your grain across the sea;
>> after many days you may receive a return. . . .
> Whoever watches the wind will not plant;
>> whoever looks at the clouds will not reap. (Eccles 11:1, 4)

But at the same time the Professor says not to put all your eggs into one basket, but to distribute the risk—which is an early mention of mutual funds! "Invest in seven ventures, yes, in eight; you do not know what disaster may come upon the land" (Eccles 11:2).

Fifth, we are to invest in eternity in the midst of our life here and now and find God in the midst of our life and work. Yet his personal exploration leads to his final conclusion in chapter 12, namely, that it is in an affectionate and reverent relationship with God—he uses the term *fear of God*—that our life makes sense or has meaning. Ecclesiastes ends where Proverbs starts: the fear of God is the beginning of wisdom. But in the context of that he hints in his exploratory research that what we do in this life can be an investment in eternity. "[God] has made everything beautiful in its time. He has also set eternity in the human heart. . . . I know that everything God does will endure forever; nothing can be added to it and nothing taken from it. God does it so that people will fear him" (Eccles 3:11, 14). This is a critical theme in Ecclesiastes and deserves careful elaboration, especially in the light of the New Testament.

2. Rewards in the New Testament. There is no word for success in the New Testament, except for the names of two women, "Success" [Euodia] and "Lucky" [Syntyche] (Phil 4:2). A better word for the goal of life in both the Old and New Testaments is *blessed* (Deut 11:26-28; Mt 5:3-12), which means "the inner riches of personal character conformed to God's character."[14] A common misunderstanding of *blessing* equates this with financial success alone. The ultimate goal for humankind in the Bible is righteousness—right relations with God, neighbor and creation. So Jesus said, "Seek first his kingdom and his righteousness" (Mt 6:33). God's evaluation of success is a scandalous inversion of human values: the widow and her mite (Mk 12:42) and the publican at prayer (Lk 18:14). If we were successful we might not know it.

We have a humble God who takes the way of downward mobility, and we are invited to follow him (Phil 2:6-11). We are to "store up for yourselves treasures in heaven" (Mt 6:20). Jesus suggests in his parable of the rich fool that the successful person (in terms of human achievement) is a stunning failure (Lk 12:20). Being "rich toward God" (Lk 12:21), the concluding words of Jesus in this story, is a challenging phrase and can easily be misunderstood. A person is not rich toward God simply by giving a lot of money to Christian causes, or even by devoting massive amounts of volunteer time to the church. One is rich toward God by investing in the kingdom of God— God's multifaceted and life-giving work in the world—by investing in relationships that will last into eternity (Lk 16:9), and by investing in heaven by doing one's work with faith, hope and love, so that in a way beyond our imagination some of our work in this life will find its way, transfigured, into the new heaven and new earth (1 Cor 3:10-15; Rev 21:24).[15] But primarily being rich toward God is hungering for and wanting God more than anything.

3. Reframing the pursuit of rewards. How to define success, being rewarded for our efforts, is a vexing question for entrepreneurs. Can a person be viewed as successful if they have built a flourishing company but have bred a dysfunctional family? One insightful source is a book written by Laura Nash and Howard Stevenson titled

---

[14]Robert Girard, "Failure," in *The Complete Book of Everyday Christianity*, p. 363.
[15]See Darrell Cosden, *The Heavenly Good of Earthly Work* (Peabody, MA: Hendrickson, 2006).

Just Enough: Tools for Creating Success in Your Work and Life,
wherein they reexamine the breadth and depth of the meaning of
success.[16] The coauthors focus on four elements of success: happiness, achievement, significance and legacy. This subsection re-
views some of the core concepts of *Just Enough.* I (Rick) also interviewed Laura Nash for her firsthand elaboration of some of the key
points in the book. Nash indicated that

> Across the board there is this enormous positive feeling that there is a
> need for a "new" definition of success. People are fed up with the greed
> and workaholic lifestyles that support today's success models. They see
> the personal stress and organizational dysfunction that has come with
> the celebrity culture. They're looking for something more lasting that
> will help them sustain multiple goals in their lives and their work.[17]

When Nash discussed a balanced approach to success among entrepreneurs and venture capitalists, there was an acknowledgment
that the one-dimensional pursuit of financial success did not make
for a contented person. At the same time, Nash was prepared for the
expected resistance to some of the book's concepts.

One typical objection is that to survive, business and entrepreneurial ventures depend on highly focused overachievers. Indeed,
sacrifice of other aspects of one's life is supposedly a sign of the real
contender's dedication, the proper ransom for the greatest reward.
These overachievers argue that "limits are for losers."[18] But there are
downsides to this approach too. "Never good enough" becomes an
addiction to work, and "less than the best" so unsatisfying as to be
not worth the effort. Nash would compare this to the kid in a race
with his friend who, upon seeing that he is losing, stops running and
claims "I wasn't trying, anyways." Admiration for these hard-charging
executives may be turning to pity as coworkers and families witness
the psychological burnout that many overachievers experience. Nash
remarked, "What surprised me is that this one-dimensional view of

---

[16]Laura Nash and Howard Stevenson, *Just Enough: Tools for Creating Success in Your
Work and Life* (New York: Wiley, 2004).
[17]Laura Nash, phone interview with Richard J. Goossen, June 16, 2004.
[18]Nash and Stevenson, *Just Enough,* p. 222.

success is becoming a minority opinion—more and more people are recognizing a broader definition of success."[19]

So the thrust of the book is that each person needs ongoing, achievable success in multiple forms. Nash and Stevenson define four important outcomes in order to generate what they refer to as "enduring success": achievement, happiness, significance and legacy. First, achievement means striving toward the extraordinary in some form. This is an ideal of excellence, an innovation, a personal stretch, an expanded capacity beyond that of your competitors without the frustration of a partial victory. Second, happiness is experiencing pleasure or contentment in and about your life. Third, significance is giving value to others, contributing something valued by society and the people you care about. Fourth, legacy is the sustained impact that will build other people's success. This is not a flash in the pan achievement but having an impact beyond your present influence on the lives of others. We are in substantial agreement with Nash and Stevenson for reasons we base on the perspective given in Scripture. Here are some of the reasons we are exploring biblically. In the Bible we are exhorted to strive for the best—the kingdom of God (excellence); we are invited to find joy in our work and life (pleasure and contentment); we are to love our neighbors (contributing something of value to others); and we are to have a lasting impact, even a multigenerational blessing (legacy). Indeed the question of legacy will be one of our closing thoughts. But the reality is that the entrepreneur is tempted in some unique ways to achieve a quick and one-dimensional success.

4. The temptations of reward seeking. There are a myriad of temptations that entrepreneurs face. Some of them come from outside (e.g., cheating and paying bribes) and some from the inside (e.g., giving in to discouragement). But the really big temptations are the very ones Jesus faced at the beginning of his ministry. They are so well known and so evocative of the real human experience that Jesus had that we fail to see they are a model of what we face in

---

[19]Nash interview.

our own callings. The fascinating and really challenging thing in the accounts of Jesus' temptations in the Gospels is that the Spirit actually led Jesus into the wilderness to be tempted by Satan. The Spirit led Jesus to be tested? Yes, there is no growth in persons without testing. That was true even in the Garden of Eden when God put a special tree as a test. So what are three of the significant temptations faced by entrepreneurs?

First, there is the temptation to cut corners to get a quick success. Jesus had been fasting for forty days and was famished, riddled with hunger. And the tempter said, "If you really are the son of God then turn these stones into bread and have a good meal" (Mt 4:3 our paraphrase). Jesus answered by quoting Deuteronomy 8, "People do not live on bread alone, but on every word that comes from the mouth of God." Many people think Jesus is saying that we should live by Scripture, which of course is a good thing to do. But in the context of Deuteronomy 8 God says that he brought Israel into the wilderness from Egypt and, he reminds them, "I fed you with manna so that you would know that human beings do not live by bread alone—that is, by what they can produce themselves—but by everything God provides, for what comes out of the mouth of God is not just words but even physical provision" (Deut 8:2-5 our paraphrase). To say that the Israelites were fed by the mouth of God or the Word of God is to say that God provided. And that is a burning issue for people in the workplace, especially in the startup phase, but often even in a well-developed enterprise that is going through a tough economic time. So the point Jesus is making is not that we must live by Scripture, as good a thing as that is, but that we can trust God to provide what we need. We can trust God for provision. So cutting corners to get this thing into success on the fast track is really a faith issue. Can we trust that God will provide what we need? But the second temptation of Jesus is just as relevant.

The devil took him to the pinnacle of the temple, at the point where, at a dizzying height, one looks down hundreds of feet to the stony ground below. "Jump off," said Satan, "and get God to rescue you. Make God act. After all, the Scripture says that you will not dash your feet against a stone since God will protect you" (Mt 4:5-6 our paraphrase). This is the temptation to force God's hand, to bet the whole farm on the project and "make" God rescue you. It is the temptation to risk everything on one project and count on God to deliver you. It is going for broke, buying Park Place and Boardwalk on the Monopoly game. And it is a faith issue. The line between trusting God and forcing God's hand, demanding that God do a miracle, is a fine line indeed, but it must be drawn. And Jesus draws it by again quoting Scripture that we must not put God to the test (Mt 4:7). That means we must not twist God's arm, force God to act in a particular way. It is a faith issue, and it happens at the very point when an entrepreneur is starting a new project or doing a major development in an existing project, when he or she is tempted to bet everything on that one effort. Entrepreneurs, particularly those starting out, sometimes naively take uncalculated risks, expecting that God would dare not allow them to fail because they have committed to tithe from their bounty to worthy causes. Even Ecclesiastes says that we should spread our investment around because we do not know whether this or that venture will actually succeed (Eccles 11:2). If the second temptation is pushing God around, as if we could, the third temptation is actually to play God ourselves.

In the third temptation the devil shows Jesus all the kingdoms of the world, the hanging gardens of Babylon and the pyramids of Egypt. And the devil says, you can have it all. You can have incredible power if you just bow down to worship me and follow my ways (Mt 4:8). This is selling out to the devil to get everything you can, getting absolute power, getting complete market share, getting control of everything and everyone by using every unscrupulous technique, compromising integrity and righteousness for the sake of job effectiveness. It is becoming your own god. The German philosopher Friedrich Nietzsche once said that if there were gods, how could he stand not to be one! And Jesus answers Satan, "You shall worship only God, nothing and no one else" (Mt 4:10 our paraphrase). This too is a faith issue, as Jesus points out. Idolatry is simply making something one's ultimate concern other than the One who is ultimate. And to worship the devil, to buy into a secular and sinful way of getting power, requires that you make something your ultimate concern other than God. And it could be yourself. In the book of Revelation, the beast from the sea controls everyone and everything (Rev 13). In the first century that beast was Caesar in the Roman Empire. In the twenty-first century the beast takes on other forms. So we are to worship—that means to give our ultimate loyalty and love—finally and fully to the living and personal God.

Resisting three alternatives, Jesus went on to the cross, the hard way. The entrepreneurial leader will often be on a hard road. Indeed there is often suffering and hardship, from financial to emotional, in starting and developing an enterprise. If we could see it all before we started we might never do it. The leader of an organization, a business or a church has to take the pain of the organization. It goes with the territory. No easy road, but it is a journey we can end well. But, as we will see, ending well has something to do with understanding our calling, the subject to which we now turn.

For Reflection and Discussion

1. Do you worship a risk-taking or a risk-averse God? What are the implications of this?

2. What is your own approach to risk? Are you risk averse, risk addicted or risk-reward analytical? Where does this come from?

3. Does your faith, or nonfaith, make you more or less cautious about taking risk?

4. Nash and Stevenson have defined success in four ways: excellence, contentment, adding value to others and having a legacy. Do you agree that these are sufficient goals for the Christian entrepreneurial leader? Why or why not? Which one is most challenging to you?

Mini Bible Study. Review the three temptations of Jesus in Matthew 4:1-11. Which one most affects you? How will you deal with it?

7

Finding Your Calling

Let each man find out what God wants him to do,
and then let him do it, or die in the attempt.

CHARLES SPURGEON

Each Christian must wrestle with and find their calling in order to fulfill God's purposes for his or her life within God's grand story. So, we ask pointedly, what are you called to? And we challenge you to answer in the personal rather than theoretical context. Have you stopped the busyness of your life to deeply examine in solitude and prayer the very meaning of your existence? A clear understanding is at the very core of being an entrepreneurial leader. If you don't have this, this chapter is for you. And if you *have* examined your sense of calling, this chapter will be a useful refresher, clarifier and motivator. It may also help you assist others to discover their callings. The task is surely a daunting one for most people, and it requires ongoing reexamination and pondering to embrace new callings as we progress through life. John Newton, author of the hymn "Amazing Grace," explained the complex process to a friend: "That which finally evidences a proper call, is a correspondent opening in providence, by a gradual train of circumstances pointing out the means, the time, the place, of actually entering upon the work."[1] Newton starts with God's role in the process; this is a fundamental distinction between the pursuit of calling, or purpose, for believers as

---

[1]John Newton, quoted in Charles Spurgeon, *Lectures to My Students* (Ross-shire, UK: Christian Focus, 1998), p. 39.

contrasted with nonbelievers. God "has saved us and called us to a holy life—not because of anything we have done but because of his own purpose and grace" (2 Tim 1:9). He has called us "according to his purpose" (Rom 8:28). "Your personal purpose is your calling—the reason you were created."[2] Our hope is that a divine calling will be an empowering reality for each reader.

In chapter three we explored the contrast of the humanist and Christian models of entrepreneurship, particularly examining the worldviews implicit in each. In this chapter we are distinguishing the humanist model and Christian model approaches on calling. It is not an easy task. As Michael Novak has observed, "The secular language of self-knowledge, identity, self-fulfillment, and the pursuit of personal happiness [all of which have contributed to the birth of the humanist model] has been so interblended with the traditional Jewish-Christian-Muslim sense of calling for thousands of years that it is not easy to pull them apart."[3]

What does it mean to be called? How is calling misunderstood? In practice do entrepreneurs understand their life and work from the perspective of calling? And how do we go about discerning our calling? These are the questions we will now explore.

What Does It Mean to Be Called?

Philip Wu in Hong Kong has done extensive research on calling from the psychological perspective.[4] Drawing on psychologists Bryan Dik and Ryan Duffy, he defined calling this way: "Calling is a transcendent summons, experienced as originating beyond the self, to approach a particular life role (e.g., work) in a manner oriented toward demonstrating or deriving a sense of purpose or meaningfulness, and that which holds other-oriented values and goals as

---

[2]Ken Blanchard and Phil Hodges, *Lead Like Jesus: Lessons from the Greatest Leadership Role Model of All Time* (Nashville: W Publishing, 2005), p. 16.
[3]Michael Novak, *Business as a Calling: Work and the Examined Life* (New York: Free Press, 1996), p. 39.
[4]Philip Wu, "Calling, Work Outcomes, & Vocational Guidance," *Creatio* 4, no. 1 (2012): 5-7, www.vocatiocreation.com.hk/unjournal.

primary sources of motivation."[5] This definition corresponds generally and remarkably with the Christian understanding of calling in which there are three dimensions.

1. Belonging to God. Without mentioning God these authors stress that calling comes from outside of the person, from a *transcendent source beyond oneself.* This is a critical component in the Christian understanding. The word *calling* invites the question "Who is calling?" For someone to be called, there must be a caller. In the Bible calling is a comprehensive summons *by* God and *to* God. The word *belonging* captures this reality. So Paul says that God has called us "into fellowship with his Son, Jesus Christ our Lord" (1 Cor 1:9). So calling is not generated from within a person but from outside, and the outside comprises not merely our parents and our society, but God.

"Bidden or not, God is present" is the epigraph of chapter four. Are only Christians called to their work? We find evidences of calling even among people who do not have a personal relationship with a transcendent God. Indeed, they will often say things like, "I was made for this." "There is an oughtness in my life and work." "This is my calling." We might ask them, "*Who* do you think is calling?" All calling is based on the reality of a God who takes initiative, who seeks to include human beings in his grand project of transforming everything. The question is whether we hear his voice, or whose voice are we listening to? But there is a second dimension of calling.

2. Being Godlike people in behavior. We are also called to a way of life. Dik and Duffy speak of this as *other-oriented values and goals as the primary source of motivation.* The calling is to life—relationships, civic responsibilities, church membership, family, neighboring and work—not just to work. Several passages in the New Testament describe our calling into a way of life. For example, "You, my brothers and sisters, were

---

[5]Philip Wu, unpublished lecture, "Empowering the People of God Through Vocational Discernment," China Graduate School of Theology, Hong Kong, May 2012. This is based on the research of B. J. Dik and R. D. Duffy, "Calling and Vocation at Work: Definitions and Prospects for Research and Practice," *Counseling Psychologist* 37 (2009): 424-50.

called to be free" (Gal 5:13). Calling language in the Bible directs people to live a life of love, hope and compassion. And therein lies one of the liberating perspectives that calling brings to the demanding and engaging task of entrepreneurship: we are called not only to invent, innovate and accomplish, but to do this in a particular way, the way of faith, hope and love, the way of justice, compassion and self-control.

3. Doing God's work in the world. Calling, according to Dik and Duffy, directs people to *approach a particular life role (e.g., work) in a manner oriented toward demonstrating or deriving a sense of purpose or meaningfulness.* Once again these researchers' definition of calling corresponds with the biblical approach. In Scripture people are called to serve God and God's purposes in the church and the world. There are multiple references to God calling people "according to his purpose" (Rom 8:28). For example, the apostle Paul writes to the whole people and not just the pastors and elders: "As a prisoner for the Lord, then, I urge you to live a life worthy of the calling you have received," after which he describes how people are to serve in the church, home and world (Eph 4:1). Further the apostle Peter states that "Each of you should use whatever gift you have received to serve others, as faithful stewards of God's grace in its various forms" (1 Pet 4:10). The English Puritans brilliantly distinguished between the "general" calling, by which people are summoned into relationship with God to become children of God, and the "particular" calling, by which people are guided into particular occupations, such as magistrate, homemaker, pastor or merchant. We may well ask, "So what?"

4. Experiencing life purpose. Calling brings meaning and purpose to our lives. Os Guinness summarizes the experience of being called in these memorable words: "Calling is the truth that God calls us to himself so decisively that everything we are, everything we do, and everything we have is invested with a special devotion, dynamism, and direction lived out as a response to his summons and service."[6] Life and work are not merely for our own advancement, not even simply to provide for our families, but we are caught up in a grand purpose, in the grand story of God's plan for creation and people. The entire notion of calling is rooted in the metanarrative of the Christian faith and subsumed by it. Ironically, it may seem, we find greater meaning and purpose in serving others and serving God than in living and working exclusively for ourselves. Philip Wu's research in Hong Kong shows that people with a sense of calling perceive a better match with their work environment, they are more satisfied with their work, their needs—social, emotional and spiritual—are more fulfilled, their interests and passions are actualized and their personal values are met.[7] But what does the Entrepreneurial Leader Research Program indicate?

The Research on Calling

Of more than 60 questions posed to approximately 250 Entrepreneurial Leaders, all with a Christian commitment, the strongest reaction—both positively and negatively—related to questions concerning whether the individual felt called to entrepreneurship. One straightforward question was posed: "Do you believe you were called to entrepreneurship?"[8] The yes group comprised 70 percent of the Entrepreneurial Leaders. Of the 30 percent that said no, there were many explanations. The no group claimed God's ongoing presence in their lives—but they did not relate this to the concept of calling. This reaction occurred even though the Entrepreneurial Leaders interviewed were selected by virtue both of their faith commitment and their commercial success.

Why did some not feel called? I (Rick) concluded from my own research that not all entrepreneurs are able to be reflective practitioners. Some said they simply needed a paycheck—and they started down the entrepreneurial path. Others said they just walked through

---

[6]Os Guinness, *The Call: Finding and Fulfilling the Central Purpose of Your Life* (Nashville: Word, 1998), p. 29.
[7]Wu, "Empowering the People of God Through Vocational Discernment."
[8]ELQ, question 21.

open doors. A few admitted the term is mainly used for pastors and missionaries.

One Entrepreneurial Leader offered the opinion that he "was gifted and led, but it was not a calling."[9] A number focused on gifts instead of calling, recognizing God's provision of specific talents or abilities, but not connecting the provision of gifts with calling. To other Entrepreneurial Leaders the term *calling* seemed too deterministic, as if everything in life was laid out in an orderly sequence. Instead, the reality of their life was a series of doors opening or opportunities arising, and they could not equate this with their view of calling. One individual in his sixties who "did not feel called" suggested that there may be different generational views of calling: "When we were young it wasn't fashionable to affirm or confirm."[10] Another individual reflected, "It was my choice; I always wanted to be my own boss. But I felt I could serve the Lord in what I was doing. The Lord maybe did call me, but I never really looked at it that way."[11] Clearly there are serious misunderstandings of calling that I uncovered in my research. It is important to explore these.

Five Misunderstandings of Calling

1. God calls only religious and spiritual workers. One of the most pernicious problems in the Christian church worldwide is the sacred-secular divide. In spite of the fact that this divide was demolished by Jesus, many churches still routinely use the language of a pastor and a missionary being called to ministry. Rarely, if ever, does anyone refer to an entrepreneur being called to the marketplace.[12] Why? Is this simply the result of bad teaching and modeling in the church, or is it actually true, as John Calvin inad-

---

[9]Rudy Loewen, quoted in *The Christian Entrepreneur: Insights from the Marketplace*, ed. Richard J. Goossen (Langley, BC: Trinity Western University, 2005–2006), 1:186.
[10]Vern Toews, quoted in *The Christian Entrepreneur*, 1:308.
[11]Peter Redekop, quoted in *The Christian Entrepreneur*, 1:252.
[12]Robert M. Anderson, quoted in *Entrepreneurial Leaders: Reflections on Faith at Work*, ed. Richard J. Goossen (Langley, BC: Trinity Western University, 2007–2010), 4:34.

vertently taught, that pastors have a special calling that sets them apart from other generally called people?[13] Our answer is the former, namely, that the church has allowed "calling" language to be associated with the clergy and professional Christians. That being said, there are reasons why Christian business and professional people are often reluctant to speak of their daily work in terms of calling.

One reason for the confusion is that while all people in the Bible are called, there is not a single instance in the New Testament of a person being called directly and supernaturally to a societal occupation such as business. By *supernaturally* we mean a transcendent experience with either an audible voice or an overwhelming conviction that they are to work in a particular occupation. But the Bible witnesses to the reality that people were drawn into significant service roles even in the Old Testament, people like Joseph, Daniel and Nehemiah, without a supernatural call. There is ample evidence that they lived out their service as called people and were providentially placed by God where they could serve strategically. In passing we note that there is also not a single instance in the New Testament of a person being called supernaturally to be a religious professional. The call of Paul on the Damascus road to become an apostle to the Gentiles is a possible exception, but this was a call to a specific service, not a call to take up a professional and remunerated religious occupation. The call to church leadership in the New Testament does not come supernaturally from God but rather from the affirmation of the people of God who identify the character and gifts needed (1 Tim 3:1-13; Tit 1:5-9). Luther claimed, rightly we think, that apostles like Paul had an unmediated call that is directly from God and not mediated by the church. For the rest, the call to church leadership is mediated and comes through the church.

So in fact God does call people to be entrepreneurial leaders, innovative leaders in church and parachurch organizations, creative

---

[13]This is dealt with in R. Paul Stevens, *The Other Six Days: Vocation, Work and Ministry in Biblical Perspective* (Grand Rapids: Eerdmans, 1999), pp. 154-55.

influencers in not-for-profit organizations. God's call in Scripture is plainly set out. Scripture proposes that human beings are called to develop the potential of creation, to embellish and improve human life, to build community on earth, to facilitate global enrichment and unity, to create wealth, to alleviate poverty, and to invest in heaven. That surely is what entrepreneurs in business do.[14] The process of discovering that call will be outlined at the end of this chapter. We can affirm that while human choices are involved in vocational discernment, ultimately it is God who summons people to relationship with God, to a way of life and to a specific task in the world for which they are uniquely fitted.

2. Calling is a one-time event. Another misunderstanding is that calling is a one-time event. Calling is a process rather than an event. Of course, it is possible that a person may have a life-changing encounter that redirects the person. Speaking in favor of this, many people rely on Old Testament narratives of the call of prophets such as Amos, Isaiah and Jeremiah. Or they may refer to Paul's life-changing and direction-setting encounter with Jesus on the Damascus road. But normally calling is experienced in degrees and over time. Michael Lindsay, in his extensive research, concludes, "Not all the people I spoke to said that they sensed a divine calling at the outset of their careers, but many described feeling 'a gradual sense of confirmation' from God."[15] Indeed many find that it is only in looking back over their life that they know they were called of God.

3. Calling has not taken place unless there is an audible voice. A number of Entrepreneurial Leaders equated calling with hearing the audible voice of God and concluded since God had not spoken to them in this way, they were not called. One Entrepreneurial Leader explained: "I think God puts opportunities in our path and sometimes we choose to take them and sometimes we

---

[14]R. Paul Stevens, *Doing God's Business: Meaning and Motivation for the Marketplace* (Grand Rapids: Eerdmans, 2006), pp. 19-39.
[15]D. Michael Lindsay, *Faith in the Halls of Power* (New York: Oxford University Press, 2007), p. 140.

don't. . . . But I cannot claim that I heard the voice of God telling me to become an entrepreneur."[16] Yet sometimes God does speak to believers in very direct ways. For example, Don Nori explained that he founded his business, Destiny Image Publishers, "due to a visitation from the Lord that called me into it. . . . It was strong enough that it lasted four days."[17] But there is another misunderstanding.

4. *Calling concerns only your occupation.* "We have jobs rather than callings" is how one Entrepreneurial Leader responded. "Called by whom? By a higher being? I cannot claim a calling or 'inspirational motivation,' except that I needed to earn a living."[18] For a number of Entrepreneurial Leaders, the basic need to have a livelihood, and in these cases as an entrepreneur, determined their career choices. They may not have sensed the overarching relevance of calling in the midst of the exigencies of earning their daily bread. This is too narrow a view, without a proper sense of perspective. Instead, as we have seen, calling is more readily identified by understanding the central themes of one's life. Calling is comprehensive concerning our relationship with God, our involvement in society, our family and friends, our civic responsibilities and our daily work.

5. *Calling is totally an individual matter.* A further contrast of the Christian model with the humanist model is the fact that the Christian view of calling must be understood within the notion of community. The call of Jesus is "inescapably a corporate calling."[19] Guinness states the paradox: "Each of us [Christians] is summoned individually and therefore uniquely and personally. But we are not summoned to be a bunch of individual believers, rather to be a community of faith."[20] This is especially true in the matter of discerning our calling, the issue to which we now turn.

---

[16]Loewen, quoted in *The Christian Entrepreneur*, p. 186.
[17]Don Nori, quoted in *Entrepreneurial Leaders,* 5:129. In addition, Nori provides a detailed explanation of this visitation at pp. 141-44; see also www.destinyimage.com/about. While only a total of 5 percent of entrepreneurial leaders interviewed cited this type of experience, it cannot be denied or minimized as a genuine possibility.
[18]Arthur Block, quoted in *The Christian Entrepreneur*, 1:52.
[19]Guinness, *Call*, p. 101.
[20]Ibid.

Vocational Discernment

Charles Spurgeon, quoted in the epigraph of this chapter, addressed the topic of calling in the context of church ministry, but with general lessons for all, which we believe has application for people in the marketplace. Spurgeon poses the question, "How may a young man know whether he is called or not?" Spurgeon fuses biblical principles with a practical bent. "The first sign of the heavenly calling is an intense, all-absorbing desire for the work." Second, "there must be aptness to teach and some measure of the qualities needful for the office of a public instructor." Third, "he must see a measure of conversion-work going on under his efforts." Fourth, "it is needful as a proof of your vocation that your preaching should be acceptable to the people of God."[21] Spurgeon argues that it would be a tragedy to spend our life in something we are not suited for and not called to.

Let's translate that into the discernment process for people called to work in the world. First, there should be an all-absorbing desire for the work. This means that God leads through the heart—motivation. Second, there must be recognition of capacity. God never calls us to a work for which he does not give us the appropriate gifts. Third, we should be able to discern some fruitfulness, some effectiveness in the direction we are going. Fourth, there needs to be affirmation from others of our suitability for a particular service.

Would that finding our calling could happen in a flash! Instead, it is a lifetime process. Most people realize they were called when they look backward. Søren Kierkegaard, the Danish philosopher, famously said, "Life is lived forward but understood backwards." Many of the responses to the research noted previously reflect this perspective. There are three critical biblical-theological principles that undergird the process of vocational discernment.

1. Biblical principles. First, God is the guide. Biblically there is no word for "guidance." That is what the ancients did in trying to figure out the will of the gods by mechanical means, reading teacups

---

[21]Spurgeon, *Lectures to My Students*, pp. 29, 30, 32, 35, 37.

and examining livers of animals and birds. It was called "divination."
We look to the Bible for guidance, and what we are given is a Guide!
Consistently the Bible is more concerned with our relationship to
the Guide than our being "in the center of his will," a concept not
actually found in the Bible but promoted by popular Christianity.
Once it is clear who guides, it is appropriate to ask how God guides.
Bruce Waltke says, "When we talk of 'finding God's will' we generally want guidance on specific choices, but it should be noted that
the term is never used after the Holy Spirit came upon the church at
Pentecost." "The New Testament," he says, "gives no command to
'find God's will,' nor can you find any instructions on how to go
about finding God's will."[22] Simply we have a Guide.

*Second, the will of God is not like a detailed blueprint but more
like an empowering vision.* Here is where a popular but profoundly
inhibiting and false teaching exists. God does not have a wonderful
plan for our lives as is often proposed, a detailed blueprint which we
must obediently follow or we will end up doing God's second best, or
worse still, not doing his will at all. God has something better than a
wonderful plan: a wonderful purpose. A plan is terrifying, especially
if we make a mistake in reading the directions. A purpose is evocative. A purpose is like a fast-flowing stream that carries us along
and allows for some mobility from side to side if we are paddling
down it in a canoe.[23] The dream God gave the young Joseph is typical
of this (Gen 37:1-11). It was a dream of greatness under God, a dream
of leadership. Though Joseph erred in trying to make it happen by
advising his brothers that they would be his servants, this dream
eventually came to pass, partly through Joseph's actions with the
jailer and with Pharaoh (Gen 39:21-23; 41:33-38).

---

[22]Bruce Waltke, *Finding the Will of God: A Pagan Idea?* (Gresham, OR: Vision House,
1995), pp. 30, 31.

[23]In the Old Testament the "will of God" is (1) God's eternal plan and decrees—his sovereign rule and unchanging counsel (Dan 4:35; Hab 2:3), (2) God's desire and consent
(Deut 10:10; Is 53:10), (3) God's general providence by which the future is in God's
hands (1 Chron 13:2), (4) God's specific choices in perplexing situations (Gen 25:22; Ex
18:15-16). In the New Testament, as well as the Old, God's will is an empowering vision
of purpose and greatness under God (Gen 37:7, 9; 12:1-3; Is 2:2-4; 49:6; Zech 9:9-10;
Jon 4; Amos 9:11-12; Acts 15:14-18).

Here is the third critical issue: vocational discernment is holistic, involving the whole person and not merely one's soul. The model we use is visualized in figure 1.

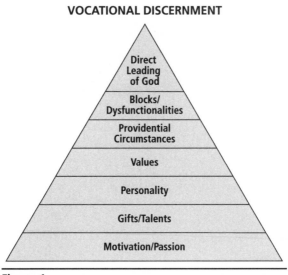

Figure 1

2. Unpacking the process. The shape of the triangle in figure 1 is significant. *At the very bottom—the largest factor—where we should start is foundational: our passions and motivations.* I (Paul) have been a "design and build" person from my infancy. As a young boy I designed and built my first boat. Later I designed and built a cabin, an education program and so on. This is not "natural." This is from God. As Elizabeth O'Connor said, "We ask to know the will of God without guessing that his will is written into our very beings."[24] What do we daydream about? In what kind of activity do we lose all sense of time? When do you feel fully alive? What are the things you obsess about, wish you had more time to put energy into? What needs doing in the world that you'd like to put your talents to work on? What activities reflect deep and consistent interests? This is from God, built into us by the Creator. Entrepreneurs typically find great joy in

---

[24]Elizabeth O'Connor, *The Eighth Day of Creation: Discovering Your Gifts and Using Them* (Waco, TX: Word, 1971), p. 15.

inventing, envisioning and bringing to birth new services and products. There is a downside to this, of course, and the growth area for many entrepreneurs is in the area of stick-to-itiveness.

Second, there are gifts and talents. God calls us by equipping us to serve in a specific way. The Entrepreneurial Leader Research Program reveals that many Entrepreneurial Leaders sense God's call through their gifts. The most commonly cited gifts, in order of frequency, are people skills, personality strengths and management skills.[25] One Entrepreneurial Leader responded: "I think I am emotionally sensitive to people. I would think that I am a person of integrity and I am a person who is willing to respond to opportunities."[26] This self-assessment is consistent with mainstream academic literature.[27] These elements are sometimes referred to as "social intelligence"—the so-called soft skills that are vital to success but which are rarely taught at business school.[28]

The third dimension of vocation discernment is our personality. This again is given by God, though it often can be emaciated through the developmental experience of childhood and young adulthood. What conversion and new birth in Christ mean is not the remaking of our personality but the release of our personalities from the paralysis of sin and the remotivation of our persons. The apostle Paul is a dramatic example of this. Before he met Christ on the Damascus road, he was a driven person, trying to find acceptance with God by his slavish keeping of the law and his oppression of heretics like the first Christians. After he met Christ he was still someone who would overcome every obstacle, but as a called person his motivation was love and gratitude. Some dimensions of personality reflected in the ELRP affirm the qualities that make an entrepreneurial leader.

Values and virtues are a further dimension of vocational discernment. While virtues are discussed further in chapter eight we

---

[25]See ELRP Analysis.

[26]Arthur DeFehr, quoted in *Entrepreneurial Leaders*, 4:106.

[27]See, for example, Jeffry A. Timmons and Stephen Spinelli, *New Venture Creation: Entrepreneurship for the 21st Century*, 8th ed. (New York: McGraw-Hill/Irwin, 2008).

[28]The best reference is the work of Daniel Goleman, *Emotional Intelligence: Why It Can Matter More Than IQ* (New York: Bantam, 1995). A follow-up book with additional insights by Goleman is *Social Intelligence: The Revolutionary New Science of Human Relationships* (New York: Bantam, 2006).

point out at this juncture the difference between virtues and values.[29] Values are cherished ways of behaving. Better still, virtues are ingrained personality traits, such as faith, hope and love, that determine how we function. Virtues, in contrast with values, have opposites—vices. And while the church has never fully adopted a formalized list of virtues from the ancient Greek world, it has emphasized in various Scriptures the fruit of the Spirit (Gal 5:22-23) and praiseworthy ways of behaving (Phil 4:8).[30] Significantly, there is a large and growing body of business literature that argues for the role of virtues in business.[31] Part of discerning the rightness of a life path is to know what values and virtues you cherish, and these may be directly given by God as well as mediated through family, society and media.

Next, moving up the triangle (see fig. 1), providential circumstances play an important part in vocational discernment. Our lives are not a bundle of accidents; God has been providentially involved in our lives, even the smallest details. This does not negate human decisiveness but means that we are not absolutely autonomous. We do not have total freedom. It is our view that Christians should be the most decisive people on earth, but they often are not, usually through fear of "not doing God's will" or of making a mistake. In chapter six we considered how our view of God determines whether we will take risks and why. But providence means that our lives are meaningful.

Here is the dictionary definition of the matter:

> Providence is the beneficent outworking of God's sovereignty whereby all events are directed and disposed to bring about those purposes of glory and good for which the universe was made. These events include the actions of free agents, which while remaining free, personal and responsible are also the intended actions of those agents.[32]

Providence is counterpoised with the following errors: deism (God

---

[29]See chap. 8, principle 2, "Making Ethical Decisions."

[30]See Iain Benson, "Values" and "Virtues," in *The Complete Book of Everyday Christianity*, ed. Robert Banks and R. Paul Stevens (Downers Grove, IL: InterVarsity Press, 1997), pp. 1064-65, 1069-72.

[31]See Clive Wright, *The Business of Virtue* (London: SPCK, 2004).

[32]*New Dictionary of Theology*, ed. S. B. Ferguson and D. F. Wright (Downers Grove, IL: InterVarsity Press, 1988), p. 541.

is detached from the present workings), fatalism (which depersonalizes human action—forces, etc.), chance and luck (providence asserts the directional and purposeful character of history). Thus even mistakes get incorporated into God's overall purpose and the weight of decision making is reduced. We are saved from arrogant egoism and cringing fear.

Blocks and dysfunctionalities are important to consider. Most people have a dark side manifested in one of the following three ways: a need to be needed, a need to have status and approval, or a need to be in control. Awareness of these needs can help us discern our calling. It can keep us from being addicted to our work, or choosing a life direction for the wrong reasons (e.g., because we gain status and approval). Each of us may have an emotional program for happiness, often compensatory for hurts and difficulties in our personal development at home. These can be discovered through contemplation and counseling, and, when identified, can become assets rather than liabilities in vocational discernment.

The final part of the vocational triangle—direct leading of God—is unfortunately what most people think is the only grounds for saying they have been called. God's call, as we have said, comes to the whole person, not just the brain or the spirit. Some people have fairly frequent direct "words" from God, but these people are rare. Such prophetic words, if one has them, may relate to a direction in Christian service in the church, but they may also relate to a societal path of service. I (Paul) have had only two such words in my lifetime, one of which was a comforting word of prophecy and the other an audible word: "You are to spend the next decade equipping the next generation."

No one, in our opinion, has been more eloquent or helpful on hearing God speak than the church mother Teresa of Ávila, the medieval reformer of a monastic movement. In her classic *Interior Castle*, she describes words from God using the term *locutions* and verifies that while occasionally God gives a spoken word as he did to Moses, most words come another way. Here is what she affirms.

Drawing on the *Medula mystica* of Francisco de Santo, Teresa says that some locutions or words come from without; they are corporeal and are heard in the ear even if no one else is able to witness the sound. Some come from the inmost parts of the soul. They are imaginary, though not in the sense of fabricated. They are not heard in the ear but experienced as an impression received by the imaginative faculty. And some locutions are intellectual and spiritual as God imprints a message in the depth of the person's spirit and understanding. Here is a critical question: How might we know that these locutions are really from God and not from Satan, or a mere figment of our own misguided imagination?

Teresa has a quiver full of wisdom on this subject. First, a message must agree with Scripture, which has power and authority. "Unless it agrees strictly with the Scriptures, take no notice of it than you would if it came from the devil himself. The words may, in fact, come only from your weak imagination . . . and must invariably be resisted so that they may gradually cease; and cease they will, because they have little power of their own."[33] Second is the sign that "a great tranquility dwells in the soul, which becomes peacefully and devoutly recollected, and ready to sing the praises of God."[34] Saint Ignatius calls this "consolation" in contrast with "desolation," the negative sign that this is not from God. The third sign is that "these words do not vanish from the memory for a very long time; some indeed never vanish at all." Teresa insists that even though others might conclude that these words are pure nonsense, and even though circumstances may militate against their fulfillment, "there still remains within it such a living spark of conviction that they will come true . . . though all other hopes may be dead, this spark of certainty could not fail to remain alive, even if the soul wished it to die."[35]

So God is the Guide. God guides and calls through the whole person. And God's will is an empowering vision that the Bible describes as advancing the kingdom of God—the unfolding of the potential of creation,

---

[33]Teresa of Ávila, *The Interior Castle*, trans. E. Allison Peers (New York: Doubleday, 1961/89), pp. 140-41.
[34]Ibid., p. 141.
[35]Ibid., p. 143.

the improvement and embellishing of human existence, the bringing of God's shalom to people and to creation, and all for the glory of God.

We want to end this chapter with a prayer for vocational discernment by Thomas Merton in his book *Thoughts in Solitude*. This deep prayer reveals and expounds the truth that while we may have a sense of being called, we are still searching for our calling.

> *My Lord God, I have no idea where I am going. I do not see the road ahead of me. I cannot know for certain where it will end. Nor do I really know myself, and the fact that I think I am following your will does not mean that I am actually doing so. But I believe that the desire to please you does in fact please you. And I hope I have that desire in all that I am doing. I hope that I will never do anything apart from that desire in all that I am doing.*
>
> *And I know that if I do this you will lead me by the right road though I may know nothing about it. Therefore will I trust you always though I may seem to be lost and in the shadow of death. I will not fear, for you are ever with me and you will never leave me to face my perils alone.*[36]

For Reflection and Discussion

1. Do some research with yourself and your coworkers on a sense of being called. Talk to them over coffee and ask about calling. How was this calling mediated? What does it mean?

2. Drawing on Kierkegaard's word, as you look backward in your life, in what ways can you discern that God has been guiding you?

3. Brood on Merton's prayer. Does this reflect a biblical viewpoint? Is it helpful? Does the lack of precision—a concrete plan for your life—trouble you? Does it increase your faith?

Mini Bible Study. Read the first of four "songs of the servant of God" in Isaiah 42:1-9. What is the servant's experience of being called? And what is the servant called to be and to do? How might this apply to servant leadership in the work world today? (Note: the

---

[36]Thomas Merton, *Thoughts in Solitude* (New York: Farrar, Straus & Giroux, 1956/58), p. 83.

Servant is one of the titles given to Jesus, since he combined the calling of being a Messiah King with being a Suffering Servant [Is 52:12–53:12; see Acts 3:26; 4:30].)

8

Practicing Entrepreneurial Leadership

We learn by doing. You learned your job on the job,
not through listening to lectures or memorizing
facts and figures. . . . We all learn through
experience, failure, and practice.

ROGER SCHANK,
COLORING OUTSIDE THE LINES

In this chapter we wish to transition from understanding and re-flection to actively doing. We urge you to begin practicing entrepreneurial leadership. What exactly is meant by the word *practice*? The *Merriam Webster Dictionary* defines *practice* as a noun with two relevant denotations: first, "actual performance or application," and second, "a systematic exercise for proficiency." On one hand, practice can mean the actual performance of the tasks. Indeed, entrepreneurship is best understood, learned and taught as a performance grounded in the realities of application. Alternatively, practice implies the ongoing drive for perfection, and persistent improvement through one's continuous focus on the process. As discussed in chapter one, entrepreneurship is primarily a practice—one focused on innovation as its core activity—and subsequently it is a craft, a wisely developed combination of experiential lessons and skills.

But is it easy to apply these principles? No. This chapter identifies the essential principles that are most common among the hundreds of Entrepreneurial Leaders that have been part of the Entrepreneurial Leader Research Program over nearly a decade.[1] The principles dis-

---

[1] ELQ, questions 36 and 37; see also ELRP Analysis.

cussed in this chapter are those the Entrepreneurial Leaders aspire to as markers of applying their faith in the marketplace. The application of these principles will lead to a life in which an individual's God-given potential is on the path to fulfillment and all aspects of one's calling are in harmony. They are intended to minimize the gap between the desire to implement the principles of Christianity and the ability to actually do so. The quest is a lifelong struggle, and entrepreneurial leaders recognize their weaknesses and propensity for failure. So, here's a starting point for becoming an entrepreneurial leader.

Principle 1: Knowing to What You Are Called

We believe that the single biggest impediment to the effectiveness of marketplace impact among Christian entrepreneurs is a lack of understanding or a misunderstanding of the Christian concept of calling. The concept of calling is discussed at length in chapter seven. While Christians have not entirely embraced the concept, the secular world has adopted its equivalencies. In mainstream management literature, the importance of identifying purpose tied into life goals is widely acknowledged and recognized. Leading management books for decades have discussed this concept, most famously in Stephen R. Covey's *Seven Habits of Highly Effective People*, with the notion of the "north star," which keeps a person pointed in the right direction. Meanwhile, in the Christian community, there is often misunderstanding, suspicion, denial and avoidance of the concept of calling. This creates a collective emaciation of the Christian business and entrepreneurial community.

There are several reasons why knowing what you are called to is so important. A clear sense of calling can lead to overwhelming conviction to stay the course of action, regardless of the challenges along the way. One example is Allan Burnett, who with his wife, Betty Ann, started a business called The Chapels.[2] They rent out wedding chapels at various scenic locales, from Vancouver, Canada, to Mexico, and also officiate at services. Allan recounted:

---

[2]See The Chapels website at www.thechapels.ca.

I really believe God has called Betty Ann and me to do what we are doing. When we go through the tough times, and when we feel like we are standing alone, we cannot forget our sense of calling. We must say to ourselves, "We are in this business because we believe it is what God has called us to do. We are going to hang on, because we know this is where we are supposed to be." We could not have gotten this far without His guidance and provision. When everyone is telling me to throw in the towel, saying, "You've gone down for the last time; stay on the mat," I want to be like Rocky in the 15th round of the fight. He looks like his face has been put through the meat grinder, yet he gets up and wins. Without that sense of calling, I would not be able to get up off the mat.[3]

Another reason knowing our call is important is that the foundation of calling is critical as a means to allow us to focus on our core purposes. John C. Maxwell explains that "people's purpose in life is always connected to their giftedness. It always works that way. You are not called to do something that you have no talent for. You will discover your purpose by finding and remaining in your strength zone."[4] Os Guinness notes that "calling directly counters the great modern pressure toward pluralization because the call of Jesus provides the priorities and perspectives that are essential for a focused life in an overloaded age."[5] Pluralization is the proliferation of choice and options, all seemingly at our fingertips, which has been exacerbated with social media and other forms of communication. Instead, we need a God-inspired focus.

The last reason for the importance of knowing what you are called to is that people are generally motivated by a hope for the future. We are called, that is, drawn to something that has not yet happened. Christians are future-oriented people. And we think of the future in a positive light. Regardless of the challenges that may come our way, we focus on an increasingly better outcome. The Bible often refers to the value of our future hope. As Proverbs notes, "Where there is no reve-

---

[3]Allan Burnett, quoted in *Entrepreneurial Leaders: Reflections on Faith and Work*, ed. Richard J. Goossen (Langley, BC: Trinity Western University, 2007–2010), 3:30.
[4]John C. Maxwell, "Self-Improvement," in *The Complete 101 Collection: What Every Leader Needs to Know* (Nashville: Thomas Nelson, 2010), p. 121.
[5]Os Guinness, *The Call* (Nashville: Word, 1998), p. 174.

lation, people cast off restraint" (Prov 29:18). There are various references in the Old Testament to the importance of hope for believers. For example, Jeremiah 29:11: "'For I know the plans I have for you,' declares the LORD, 'plans to prosper you and not to harm you, plans to give you hope and a future.'" In short, the clearer the concept of calling, the more invigorating should be our vision for the future.

Principle 2: Making Ethical Decisions

Historically there is Christian commentary against involvement in business—it is likened to voluntarily jumping into an ethical cesspool. Some grunge will surely stick—it's only a question of how much. An ethical approach to life is a challenge for any believer, but possibly more so for those in business, and even doubly so for entrepreneurs. Why? Those in business may face challenges within the guidelines set by their employer. Entrepreneurs, however, largely set their own parameters without any oversight or consultation— and being action oriented they often put a premium on moving ahead before thinking through all the consequences of their actions. As one Entrepreneurial Leader explained,

> The most significant challenges are the temptations to do wrong when nobody will see you doing wrong. That's the most difficult thing. You sit behind that desk and things cross your desk that you could do and nobody would see it. Nobody would know except, of course, the Lord. You have to have a vibrant enough understanding of God's presence that you resist those temptations.[6]

Susceptibility to temptations to act unethically is exacerbated because those who aren't honest often appear to do just fine. A seminal article coauthored by Howard Stevenson, professor of entrepreneurship at Harvard Business School, is provocatively titled "Why Be Honest If Honesty Doesn't Pay?"[7] His conclusion in the article is that honesty typically doesn't pay. I (Rick) interviewed Howard Stevenson specifically on ethics in relation to entrepreneurship. While Stevenson's ar-

---

[6]Don Nori, quoted in *Entrepreneurial Leaders*, 5:138.
[7]Amar Bhide and Howard H. Stevenson, "Why Be Honest If Honesty Doesn't Pay?" *Harvard Business Review*, September-October 1990, pp. 121-29.

ticle revealed that dishonest people can and do succeed, he believes intuitively that this is short-term oriented and that ethics are absolutely critical to sustainable entrepreneurial success. Stevenson explains that, "It's absolutely critical that they have a sense of ethics and a sense of proportion and dealing with other people. That doesn't mean you can't succeed by cheating and that stuff, because clearly I'd be naive to say you can't."[8] However, as entrepreneurs interact with a wide variety of people, going out to raise money for people, for example, there must be an implicit and explicit sense of trust among those people. In fact, honesty does not pay in the short term but may pay in the long term.

Entrepreneurs face different or unique ethical challenges in comparison to company managers. Stevenson noted, "I think you are faced with more opportunities and more pressure. For many entrepreneurs, when things are going badly, there's always the chance to think about whether they should cut just a little closer to the line."[9] The pressures on the entrepreneur may not be from the outside. Because of the unique dynamics of the entrepreneurial process, there are pressures arising from the individual risks undertaken, especially when things do not work out. Stevenson points out, however, that most of the entrepreneurs who succeed in the long run actually do have a very strong sense of ethics because "they know that ultimately their ability to do a deal twice depends on treating people fairly the first time." What is the framework for approaching the marketplace?

We believe that a focus on Christian virtues is the proper starting point. Richard W. Higginson of Ridley Hall, University of Cambridge, explains that "'follow the rules' and 'calculate consequences' [utilitarian approach] are being seen as increasingly unsatisfactory answers to the question of how we should make moral decisions. In contrast, the virtue approach focuses on what we are, believing this will ultimately take care of what we do. This approach has much to commend it from a Christian perspective."[10]

---

[8]Howard Stevenson, phone interview with Richard J. Goossen, August 8, 2005.
[9]Ibid.
[10]Richard W. Higginson, "Virtues in Business," Ridley Hall, Cambridge, www.ridley.cam.ac.uk/documents/fib/virtues.html.

Theodore Malloch of Yale University views virtue as at the core of the work of business people and entrepreneurs.[11] Malloch distinguishes between rule-guided conduct, such as with Kant (duty is at the heart of moral thinking), and a moral life based on virtue. Virtue refers to ingrained character traits—not what you do but what you are.[12] For our purposes we commend a virtue-based approach; while the law reflects a deontological approach, Jesus teaches us through virtues to go beyond it. This is not easy. N. T. Wright notes that "The key to virtue lies precisely . . . in the transformation of the mind."[13]

One example of a virtue-based approach is reflected in how one Entrepreneurial Leader, Volker Wagner, handled an ethical challenge. Wagner has a Vancouver-based publishing company, which sells products throughout North America. He recounts his ill-fated expansion into Australia: "When Teldon Australia went into receivership on November 1, 2004, my wife and I wrote letters to the suppliers the company owed money to: we offered to personally pay them 63% of any shortfall they would experience."[14] This 63 percent reflected their personal shareholdings in Teldon Australia. Ultimately the receiver paid out 38 percent to all unsecured suppliers, leaving investors with a shortfall. Wagner explains that "my wife and I joyfully issued cheques as promised, although there was no legal obligation to do so. This was our expression of honoring Jesus Christ and living up to our commitments." This was a challenging thing to do, beyond the norms le-

---

[11]For more information see Center for Faith and Culture, Yale Divinity School (www .yale.edu/faith).

[12]Theodore Roosevelt Malloch, *Spiritual Enterprise: Doing Virtuous Business* (New York: Encounter Books, 2008), p. 18. Malloch lists the virtues of business: faith, honesty, gratitude, perseverance, compassion, forgiveness, patience, humility, courage, respect, generosity, discipline, chastity, thrift (pp. 27-35). The three cardinal virtues of business are creativity, building community and practical realism (p. 36). He distinguishes between "hard virtues" (leadership, courage, patience, perseverance and discipline) and "soft virtues" (justice, compassion, forgiveness, gratitude and humility), which temper the hard virtues (p. 77).

[13]N. T. Wright, *After You Believe: Why Christian Character Matters* (New York: Harper Collins, 2010), p. 259.

[14]Volker Wagner, quoted in *Entrepreneurial Leaders*, 3:223-24.

gally required, but the virtues of his faith compelled him to do so. This type of approach practiced on a consistent basis leads to another principle.

Principle 3: Practicing Integrity

Ethical actions practiced consistently result in a reputation for integrity. This can be phrased different ways: your word is your bond, you do what you say, you can be counted on. The bottom line is that those who deal with you have confidence that they can trust you. Business is based on trust. Principle 3 is part and parcel of the previous section on ethics—but it is an elaboration. We briefly discussed various approaches to ethics, including the virtue theory. The core concept is that the person acts based on internal beliefs rather than external dictates.

Entrepreneurial Leaders, as noted, frequently referenced integrity in the context of the overall approach to the marketplace. Jim Pattison, for example, listed his priorities for ethical decision making: "The lessons are no different for a Christian or non-Christian. First, integrity is very important. You have got to be honest. Second, you have to persevere when things don't go your way. And it's important to be optimistic. Third, you need to work hard."[15] Integrity also means having your actions match your words. Dale Lutz, a software company founder, notes the importance of integrity not just for the individual but for the greater community:

> As a Christian entrepreneur I believe I do carry a little bit heavier load because I am in more of a position of influence and power in people's lives or in terms of other dealings. You can do a lot of damage to the Christian reputation and so, in a way, you have to be consistent and walk the walk a lot more carefully than if you weren't an entrepreneur. So, I believe there is a great responsibility to project your faith well through your actions. I think those high-profile Christians who falter can set back the reputation of Christians greatly.[16]

---

[15]Jim Pattison, phone interview with Richard J. Goossen, October 6, 2005.
[16]Dale Lutz interview, June 17, 2011, www.eleaders.org/qry/page.taf?id=54.

John Lovatt, founder of Acme Projects, Stoke-on-Trent, England, recounted his most triumphant moment as relating to an event when he was in Tangshan, China. He was negotiating for a new contract with a factory to build new sanitary ware kilns. He visited an old customer who told him that the prospective customer had sent a delegation to them with the message that they had never done business with the English, and what was their opinion of Acme? He told him that they replied, "These people can be trusted, they do as they say."[17] Lovatt got the order. Lovatt took this to be a great affirmation of the integrity—or trustworthiness—of him and his company.

Art DeFehr has been in business for almost fifty years and has had up to three thousand people working for his furniture-manufacturing company. He notes that "Christians pursuing entrepreneurship need to be honest and consistent. If you are a Christian, people will judge your actions and style." He further explains that "trust matters a lot over time. Being a good Christian means doing things with and for others, being consistent, and having good relationships."[18] How does this come about? The next principle addresses this issue.

Principle 4: Engaging in Spiritual Disciplines

Richard Foster, author of *Celebration of Discipline*, notes that spiritual disciplines "allow us to place ourselves before God so that He can transform us."[19] Interestingly, the role of spiritual disciplines arose not in response to a specific question in the ELQ but rather a general question on lessons that are important for others pursuing entrepreneurship. By *spiritual disciplines* we are referring to matters such as prayer, meditation, reflection and contemplation. The outcome of spiritual disciplines is to strive for a Christ-centered, balanced life. This is beyond the introspection and self-reflection that any thoughtful entre-

---

[17]John Lovatt, quoted in *Entrepreneurial Leaders*, 4:210.
[18]Arthur DeFehr, quoted in ibid., 4:109.
[19]Richard Foster, *Celebration of Discipline: The Path to Spiritual Growth* (New York: Harper & Row, 1978), p. 6. See Foster for a detailed discussion of spiritual disciplines.

preneur should pursue regardless of a faith perspective. Instead, Christian entrepreneurial leaders strive to seek wisdom from the Bible and related materials, alone and in fellowship with others.

Charles Loewen, CEO and board chair of Loewen Windows, with fifteen hundred employees, is a major manufacturer of windows for markets throughout North America. Loewen notes, "Don't get seduced by power and money. Retain spiritual disciplines. . . . There are times when my Sunday school class is really important to me and there are times when my Christian business colleagues are important to me, and there are times when reading spiritual resources, meditating and prayer is important to me."[20]

Where do Entrepreneurial Leaders look for inspiration in their spiritual disciplines? One example is John Lovatt, who finds inspiration regarding some fundamental principles from four classic Christian thinkers. The first is Martin Luther (1483-1546), who reminds Lovatt to be honest. When faced with being thrown out of the church, losing his job and income, and possibly death unless he recanted (i.e., denied his beliefs contrary to the Roman Catholic Church), Luther said: "my conscience is captive to the Word of God. I cannot and I will not recant anything, for to go against conscience is neither right nor safe. Here I stand, I cannot do otherwise, God help me. Amen." Lovatt notes that "This has inspired many, including me, to stick to what they believe is right and true."[21]

The second thinker is St. Francis of Assisi (1181-1226), who inspires Lovatt to forgive. He explains, "In business, we have to put up with injustices, insults, being misunderstood, and being generally badly treated. Forgiving is not easy. There is a lovely story in *The Little Flowers of St. Francis*, written a hundred years after Francis' death, called 'Perfect Joy' (II:8). Francis teases his companion Leo that healing powers, deep learning, or evangelisation gifts do not give joy: true joy comes from being insulted and turned away, and

---

[20]Charles Loewen, quoted in *The Christian Entrepreneur: Insights from the Marketplace*, ed. Richard J. Goossen (Langley, BC: Trinity Western University, 2005–2006), 1:174. Since the time of the interview, Loewen has sold the business but remains involved in an advisory capacity.

[21]Lovatt, quoted in *Entrepreneurial Leaders*, 4:215.

'accepting this with love and joy in our hearts.'"[22]

A third thinker who influenced Lovatt is John Wesley (1703-1791). Wesley, an Anglican minister and Christian theologian, was an early leader in the Methodist movement. His Sermon 44 on "The Use of Money" contains three themes: "First, Gain all you can, Second, Save all you can, Third, Give all you can." By "gain," Wesley means "make money."[23] Lovatt explains that "This sermon inspired me to be confident about trying to make a profit, because without profits, you cannot save enough to make the business secure, nor indeed give away profits to charity or in tax."[24]

The fourth thinker was John Bunyan (1628-1688). Bunyan was an English preacher and writer. While imprisoned for preaching the gospel without receiving permission from the Anglican Church, he wrote the classic *Pilgrim's Progress*. Lovatt comments that Bunyan "was able to forgive and suffer in prison, without resentment to his captors, and make the suffering a way of producing such an inspired book."[25]

Prayer is cited as vitally important in many Christ-centered businesses. Terry Smith, chairman of Smiths Gardens, which operates in Washington and California, maintains spiritual disciplines for the company. Terry explains that

> I have always believed that my business was entrusted to me by God. I have tried to implement biblical principles in every aspect of the company, so I would find it hard to separate the secular from the sacred. I have made all my plans while counting on God to direct my steps. This dependence on God has given me great peace of mind. Today, more than ever, I realize I am merely a steward of what God has blessed me with.[26]

One hoped-for outcome of practicing spiritual disciplines is that we have a proper view of ourselves.

---

[22]Ibid.

[23]John Wesley, "The Use of Money," in *On Moral Business: Classical and Contemporary Resources for Ethics in Economic Life*, ed. Max L. Stackhouse et al. (Grand Rapids: Eerdmans, 1995), pp. 194-97.

[24]Lovatt, quoted in *Entrepreneurial Leaders*, 4:215.

[25]Ibid.

[26]Terry Smith, quoted in *Entrepreneurial Leaders*, 3:169.

Principle 5: Managing Your Own Ego

N. T. Wright eloquently states, "the deadliest snake of all, pride, is always lurking in the long grass, ready to bite those who fancy themselves effortlessly superior to their disadvantaged neighbours."[27] This sentiment is echoed in the corridors of leading business schools. Harvard professor Howard Stevenson emphasized this approach in my (Rick's) interview with him. "I think almost all people who are successful have an understanding that it's about more than them."[28] He stressed that success should not be achieved through personal aggrandizement. An orientation to the needs of others will serve entrepreneurs best in the long term. This concept is extended in many ways. Entrepreneurs often look for "low ego" among potential new hires.

While low ego and being other-centered is cited in general entrepreneurial circles as a good tip for success, in the context of our discussion there is a spiritual impetus. The most-quoted verse among Entrepreneurial Leaders is Micah 6:8:

> He has shown all you people what is good.
> And what does the LORD require of you?
> To act justly and to love mercy
> and *to walk humbly with your God*. (emphasis added)

The old hymn "When I Survey the Wondrous Cross" has the refrain of "pour contempt on all my pride." John Lovatt cautions, "Beware the sense of power. It is essential to be humble and to listen to your staff, following their needs and ideas."[29] The comments vary among Entrepreneurial Leaders, but they all have the same thrust: be modest, don't dwell on self, don't be too proud to accept advice, realize your good fortune and so forth.

Entrepreneurial Leaders generally recognize that their success does not come solely from their own efforts. There are too many other factors, such as the big picture of economics and market timing, to warrant taking full credit. Entrepreneurial leaders are

---

[27]N. T. Wright, *After You Believe*, p. 205.
[28]Howard Stevenson, quoted in *Entrepreneurial Excellence: Profit from the Best Ideas of the Experts*, ed. Richard Goossen (Franklin Lakes, NJ: Career Press, 2007), p. 153.
[29]Lovatt, quoted in *Entrepreneurial Leaders*, 4:214.

likely to echo the words of John Bradford (1510-1555), an English Reformer and martyr, who uttered, "There but for the grace of God goes John Bradford" while imprisoned in the Tower of London as he saw a criminal heading to his execution. There is humility that is an outgrowth of an understanding of the complexities of the marketplace—fortunes can change quickly.

Dale Lutz, a software company founder, explains,

> Because of my faith, I do not view my company's success as caused solely by me. My success is because God has chosen to bless me, my partner and the people in my company. I think it would be very easy as a non-Christian entrepreneur to be very full of themselves. The Christian faith, for me, is a lot to do with keeping humble. I think that's one side of that.[30]

There is a relevant reference in the Old Testament: "But remember the LORD your God, for it is he who gives you the ability to produce wealth, and so confirms his covenant, which he swore to your ancestors, as it is today" (Deut 8:18).

Ego management also relates to entrepreneurs' roles in their companies. They should not build the company around themselves. They should strive to keep their life in balance and not put themselves at the center of this small, commercial universe. This is not easily done, but there is the spiritual imperative not to think of our own self-importance and to subsume everything to that. Often the self-important person is reflected in a severe work imbalance. This last comment points to a further principle.

Principle 6: Seeking Wise Counsel

Entrepreneurs typically have great confidence in their own ability; this is often reinforced as their very success has often come by proving naysayers wrong. This approach, however, rarely provides long-term success. As a general rule, entrepreneurs should seriously consider the insights of others. Entrepreneurs can benefit from a

---

[30]Dale Lutz, interviewed by Richard J. Goossen, June 17, 2011, www.eleaders.org/qry/page.taf?id=54.

board of directors or advisers that provide a wide range of supplementary expertise, broad experience and a range of contacts.[31] Other important sources of guidance come from professional advisers such as lawyers, accountants and bankers. Entrepreneurs should also seek and benefit from the input of peers. These could be individuals in the same industry. Or the peers could be a collection of founders/CEOs in different industries, but at the same stage of growth in the life cycle of their firm.

Christians should seek out other Christians for in-depth fellowship, where they can share their deepest concerns. As Proverbs notes, "Plans fail for lack of counsel, but with many advisers they succeed" (Prov 15:22). Where can entrepreneurs find wise counsel? Entrepreneurial Leaders were asked, "Who was most helpful (and why or how) in addressing these challenges: church leadership, Christian friends, etc.?"[32] When addressing issues regarding how to face challenges of faith and business integration, most entrepreneurs look to friends first. One Entrepreneurial Leader noted, "My Christian friends have been helpful in addressing the challenges of business. In our Bible study, a group of businessmen meet and we talk about those challenges and that has been very supportive."[33] Another concurring Entrepreneurial Leader was Ian Daniel of NCOL Internet, a web design firm with clients throughout North America. Daniel explained:

> My sense of direction has been affirmed by a Christian mentor and Christian friends. I meet with a group of guys early on Wednesday mornings and I have been meeting with them since before I was married. I bounce a lot of things off those guys. We hold each other accountable and ask difficult questions. We know each other very well after all these years. I think of them as my advisory board in many ways.[34]

---

[31]Leading academic research indicates that entrepreneurs benefit from moral support networks (family and friends) and professional support networks (business associates and trade associations). See Robert Hisrich, Michael Peters and Dean Shepherd, *Entrepreneurship*, 9th ed. (New York: McGraw-Hill/Irwin, 2013), p. 20.
[32]ELQ, question 40.
[33]Richard Coleman, quoted in *The Christian Entrepreneur*, 1:78.
[34]Ian Daniel, quoted in *Entrepreneurial Leaders*, 5:31.

Rarely did these Entrepreneurial Leaders receive support from only one source.

The second most helpful source revealed in the research was church leadership. The church typically played an important role due to the particular expertise or experience of the pastor, rather than an institutional or board decision to deliberately pursue marketplace ministries. The pastors praised for their ministries often had experience in business or entrepreneurship, and entered the pastorate in their thirties or forties rather than directly out of post-secondary training.

Closely behind the church, Entrepreneurial Leaders cited the support of family. Often a spouse was credited with providing the greatest support. One-time billionaire Ray Loewen explained:

> My wife has been the most helpful person in my life. While an entrepreneur may appear to be gregarious, they are often quiet individuals. So I would say my wife, family, and a few friends were most helpful in addressing the challenges of practicing my faith in business—and the more successful we got, the smaller this circle became.[35]

As his company, Loewen Funeral Homes, kept growing in size and name recognition, everyone's motives were questionable. The next principle turns the relationship factor inside out—not how we get support but how we give it.

Principle 7: Abiding by the Golden Rule

"He who has the gold, makes the rules" is not the Golden Rule we are talking about! Instead, we are focused on "Do to others what you would have them do to you" (Mt 7:12). You can't go too far wrong, goes common wisdom, by simply treating others as you would like to be treated. General entrepreneurial writings are replete with reference to this principle. For our purposes I will only cite one source. Daniel Goleman, author of *Emotional Intelligence*, has captured the essence of how some people are successful while others are not. Goleman concludes, "The most effective leaders are alike in one

---

[35]Ray Loewen, quoted in *The Christian Entrepreneur*, 2:244.

crucial way: they all have a high degree of what has come to be known as emotional intelligence."[36] He explains that his research "clearly shows that emotional intelligence is the *sine qua non* of leadership."[37] This is not to say, of course, that intellectual ability is irrelevant. Rather, Goleman's conclusion is that emotional intelligence has been a traditionally little understood and neglected part of comprehending factors for success.[38] He identifies five components of emotional intelligence, one of which is "social skills." Goleman defines social skills as proficiency in managing relationships and building networks, and an ability to find common ground and build rapport.[39]

The Entrepreneurial Leader Research Program likewise recognized the importance of social skills. When Entrepreneurial Leaders were asked, "What have been the biggest challenges for you as a Christian in business?" one of the three most-commonly cited responses was "people issues."[40] Entrepreneurial Leaders routinely mentioned the importance of interpersonal skills as critical to their success. In fact, almost all of them would be viewed as having a high degree of so-called people skills despite the challenges in managing and leading a work force. While from a secular standpoint social skills are important, from a Christian perspective we should take seriously the biblical mandate to treat all people—whether customers or employees—with fairness, dignity and respect, as we ourselves want to be treated. Of course, the challenges come with the practical application of this concept. Entrepreneurial Leaders are quite clear that a business must be financially viable or there will be no livelihood for anyone. Further, if someone is not able to make a valuable contribution, they should not be part of the enterprise. Issues arise on many fronts due to common misunderstandings.

---

[36]Daniel Goleman, *Emotional Intelligence: Why It Can Matter More Than IQ* (New York: Bantam, 1995), p. 94.
[37]Ibid.
[38]Daniel Goleman, "What Makes a Leader?" *Harvard Business Review*, November-December 1998, pp. 93-102.
[39]Goleman, *Emotional Intelligence*, p. 94.
[40]ELQ, question 39.

Someone may be hired from within the church, possibly even a relative of a pastor, and then it may not work out. In some cases the person may think they do not have to work as hard as others. Or they may think that their boss, as a Christian, should be forgiving of transgressions and extend the hand of grace. Interestingly, these people seem very clear that this is a proper use of grace. But in fact the person may merit dismissal. Is this un-Christian? No, but it creates problems because of different levels of sophistication when dealing with faith and business issues.

Entrepreneurial leaders need to tread carefully with people. One Entrepreneurial Leader, Dale Lutz of Safe Software, recognizes the challenges of honing good people skills. He acknowledges that "You are going to find yourself in situations where doing the Christian thing is going to be uncomfortable from time to time and you have to ready yourself for that and still be ready to make that decision. . . . I think the development of a Christian approach around dealing with employees is a big issue."[41] Lutz recognizes that while the employer makes the final decision, they need to do so deftly. He observes,

> People—all of us—are flawed. I am flawed and sometimes employees are flawed. You put some of those flaws together and there will be situations that aren't easy, and so reconciling that and having the strength to recognize when you are at fault and having a low enough ego yourself to accept it. At the same time, when others are at fault, you need to be able to work through that.[42]

Those are difficult areas that require wisdom to resolve in a transparent manner.

In conclusion, this chapter offered seven principles for developing spiritual maturity through practicing entrepreneurial leadership in the marketplace. These have encompassed motivation (being called), behavior (ethics and integrity), resources (spiritual disciplines), self-understanding (ego), support (wise counsel) and relationships (the Golden Rule). In chapter nine we are considering

---

[41]Dale Lutz interview.
[42]Ibid.

yet one more dimension of entrepreneurial leaders: how to sustain the practice of Christian entrepreneurial leadership in the workplace. Further, how to not only sustain it but to go beyond that and view it as a ministry. It is part of a much bigger issue of the current language of "business as mission," a subject which both authors have explored in theory and practice.

For Reflection and Discussion

Choose one of the principles of this chapter that challenged you. Share it with someone else, possibly a colleague or a spouse. Do you want to grow in this area? Can you ask someone to hold you accountable in this area of your life?

Mini Bible Study. In one case in this chapter, that of Volker Wagner, the person went beyond what was required by law. Read Matthew 5:17-20 and Luke 17:7-10. In terms of ethical business dealing, is it practical to live by the teaching of Jesus to exceed the law keeping of the scribes and Pharisees and merely doing your duty? Is this exceptional or normal? Why?

9

Sustaining Entrepreneurial Leadership

The commercial business marketplace may
well be the primary mission field
of the twenty-first century.

CHARLES VAN ENGEN

In this chapter we are making three grand assumptions. The first assumption is that you the reader are a person of faith and that you want to integrate your faith in your work. Rather than keeping your faith and work in separate compartments—Sunday religion—we assume you wish to be a consistent person all week long. The second assumption is based on our conviction that there is no part-time ministry available for followers of Jesus. As we have seen earlier, all of God's people are doing "the work of the Lord," whether that work is creating, sustaining, transforming or bringing things to a conclusion. The third assumption is a big one: You do not want to be silent about your faith. You want to share it in word and deed. Indeed, as the epigraph to this chapter suggests, the marketplace is both part of the mission of God to bring transformation into the world and also a mission field in which we can announce the good news of the kingdom of God to others.[1] But how? And what are we likely to face as we do this? In this chapter we will develop seven principles of overcoming

---

[1]A development of the theology and practice of marketplace mission is found in R. Paul Stevens, *Doing God's Business: Meaning and Motivation for the Marketplace* (Grand Rapids: Eerdmans, 2006), pp. 78-100.

the challenges that, based on our research, are quite common among entrepreneurs. But we must start with articulating the faith.

Principle 1: Sharing Faith Responsibly

We live and work in a diversified, pluralistic society. But it is a world to be reached with the good news. A majority of Entrepreneurial Leaders view their business as a mission field. One individual stated unequivocally, "Yes . . . I believe that the marketplace is something that God calls men and women to, just like he does to a mission field."[2] One of the Entrepreneurial Leaders echoed this sentiment through the following mission statement on his company's website: "Our Company exists to glorify God. We seek to do so by providing exceptional service to our customers, by creating wealth for those who labor in Remdal [Painting & Restoration Ltd.] and by fostering growth and maturity in the lives of others."[3] And yet there are challenges. As one Entrepreneurial Leader confided, "I think the biggest challenge for me is to know when to speak of Christ and when to be silent and wait to be asked."[4] In work environments with many different worldviews, how do entrepreneurial leaders share their faith within their company's workforce?

In today's age it seems both politically incorrect and legally dangerous to attempt to share faith through one's company. With respect to the former, today's society, especially in the post-Christian West, would view any claims of one religion providing answers as passé; the notion of trying to foist one's views on another seems outmoded. Ian Mitroff and Elisabeth Denton, cited extensively in chapter four, state: "Because Western societies are extremely wary of false religions in disguise, and rightly so, the leaders of organizations are forewarned not to promote anything that smacks of religion." Mitroff and Denton conclude that "Spirituality is best attained through gentleness and softness" and suggest "not to cram spirituality down the throats of

---

[2]Keith Richardson, quoted in *The Christian Entrepreneur: Insights from the Marketplace*, ed. Richard J. Goossen (Langley, BC: Trinity Western University, 2005–2006), 1:279.
[3]Ken Ewert, quoted in ibid. See www.remdal.com/remdal09/about/mission.html.
[4]Ben Wendland, quoted in *The Christian Entrepreneur*, 2:404.

individuals or organizations as a whole."[5] The Entrepreneurial Leader Research Program indicates that this is, indeed, the approach of the majority of Entrepreneurial Leaders.

There are many examples of Entrepreneurial Leaders being very transparent about their faith. One example is Esther de Wolde of Phantom Screens, who has always been clear about the purpose of her business: "I've always been wired to see the workplace as a ministry."[6] She grew up in a home where her parents were very transparent about their faith. When she and her partners started Phantom, their corporate values reflected their will to honor God in all they did. She explains, "We built our business on a foundation that if it was not God honoring, we would not take part in it."[7] Another Entrepreneurial Leader is John Fluevog, whose shoes are worn by celebrities worldwide. He explains his balanced approach:

> I put messages on my shoes and on my website, but I'm careful not to be too preachy. It's not about preaching to people or giving them your morality. But the cool thing about being in business for yourself is that you do not need to be politically correct. . . . I can do exactly what I want. We are in a unique time in which Christians can influence. That's why I think being an entrepreneur is such a unique thing—it is a vehicle to express yourself.[8]

Let's look in more detail at how Entrepreneurial Leaders balance sharing faith appropriately. An example of a balanced approach is Ben Sawatzky, founder of Spruceland Lumber: "I have had a personal prayer for over 20 years that I would be given an opportunity to lead one of my employees to the Lord every year. It hasn't happened every year but it's happened many, many years and sometimes more than once. I always wait for them to come to me."[9] His

---

[5]Ian I. Mitroff and Elisabeth A. Denton, *A Spiritual Audit of Corporate America: A Hard Look at Spirituality, Religion and Values in the Workplace* (San Francisco: Jossey-Bass, 1999), p. 184.

[6]Esther de Wolde, quoted in *Entrepreneurial Leaders: Reflections on Faith and Work*, ed. Richard J. Goossen (Langley, BC: Trinity Western University, 2007–2010), 4:124-25.

[7]Ibid.

[8]John Fluevog, quoted in *The Christian Entrepreneur*, 2:177-78.

[9]Ben Sawatzky, quoted in *Entrepreneurial Leaders*, 5:199-200.

prayer is that they would come to him for advice without him pushing his advice on them. He never wants to forgo an opportunity to share his faith. He explains, "When we have our year end party—which we call a Christmas party in this company—I never forgo an opportunity to tell people what Christmas means to me."[10]

Sawatzky explains one of his opportunities to share his faith. In recent years, he has told employees about his personal charitable activities. He had kept his activities confidential for a number of years, but then he went public with it because employees had asked. His employees are largely representative of Canadian society, with probably only 7-8 percent of his workforce who are evangelical Christians. He shared that he was involved with the construction of an orphanage in Kenya and a village for the homeless Haitians in the Dominican Republic. He explained that "if you are really interested and if you would consider donating one hour per week of your pay, you could do this for the orphanages, you could do this for the village in the Dominican Republic, and by the way in the middle of your tables there are some questionnaires which you can fill out and hand in to your supervisor who'll bring it to the personnel office next week and you can start being a part of it."[11] As a result, 78 percent of his employees started donating money to these causes. Sawatzky makes it clear to his employees what motivates his philanthropic initiatives.

A workplace must be an open environment, and the notion of a boss espousing a particular religion, and encouraging others within the workplace to adopt that religion, would easily lead to charges that an employee could be denied opportunities due to not going along with those entreaties. Being the owner/entrepreneur is legally quite distinct from being an employee. Entrepreneurial leaders need to strike a fine balance of being faith motivated while not being manipulative, respectful but not compromising, transparent but not domineering, abiding by the law but not being restricted by the law. A deft touch when handling the issue of how to share faith respon-

---

[10]Ibid.
[11]Ibid.

sibly will have a significant impact for good in the marketplace. But how do we avoid a lack of integrity with respect to our faith? Or can we?

Principle 2: Avoiding Hypocrisy

We call it the "H word." Non-Christians revel in pointing out the hypocrisy of Christians, whether tales of TV evangelists' infidelities or a high-level Christian entrepreneur who defrauds his company. Christians, too, frequently look for ways to poke holes in the spiritual armor of their fellow believers. Some individuals that I (Rick) asked to be interviewed as part of the ELRP huffed that if "so-and-so" was included, then the entire credibility of the project was undermined and they would not deign to be included. Other entrepreneurs, who I know had a great story to tell, chose not to be included because they thought they would be perceived as a self-righteous example for others to emulate.[12] The specter of public labeling as a hypocrite dissuaded a number of individuals from sharing their entrepreneurial experiences.

The charge of hypocrisy cuts deeply. For an individual who professes faith and is doing their best in difficult circumstances, public exposure as someone who essentially does not do what he or she says, or in fact be what he or she is trying to appear to be, goes to the core of the person's being. This issue is particularly acute for entrepreneurs, who typically cast a wide net of relationships throughout a business community in order to start up and maintain a business. Paul Fast, of Fast + Epp Engineers, explains:

> If you do work that is lousy, or if you're not on time—not that we're all perfect—but if you're consistently not on time, or if you're lacking in integrity in your business, don't go and tell people about Christ and what He can do for you. There has to be a deep desire to want to do excellent work. . . . It's also important that when you do fall short, you

---

[12]Jesus said, when confronting the accusers of the woman caught in adultery, "Let any one of you who is without sin be the first to throw a stone at her" (Jn 8:7). In a similar way, entrepreneurs often don't want to point out how others should act when they realize they may be falling short.

acknowledge it. That goes a long way towards making things good and preserving a good reputation.[13]

The Christian entrepreneurial leader who is active in the market-place will probably have the hypocrisy charge hurled early and often. If that doesn't happen, then the leader may not be pushing his or her witness. Why? Often Christians who are overly concerned with crit-icism end up having little or no impact in the marketplace. They are governed by what people might think, rather than doing the right thing. If you don't let people know you are a Christian, then no one will call you a hypocrite, because they don't think you are aspiring to live up to any particular standards.

Principle 3: Dealing with Betrayal

"Christian" is the protagonist in John Bunyan's allegory *Pilgrim's Progress*, which is centered on Christian's journey from his hometown of "City of Destruction" to "Celestial City." Christian comes across various characters along the way. The characters are obvious to us—by their adjectival naming—but not obvious to Christian. One character named "Honest" cautions Christian: "It happens to us as it happeneth to wayfaring men: sometimes our way is clean, sometimes foul; sometimes up hill, sometimes down hill; we are seldom at a certainty. The wind is not always at our backs; nor is everyone a friend we meet with in the way."[14] These people— just like the individuals met by entrepreneurial leaders—serve to distract Christian from completing his journey. A person who ap-pears to be a friend may not be one. This is the experience of many Entrepreneurial Leaders.

There was silence at the other end of the phone line. After interviews with approximately 250 Entrepreneurial Leaders I had come to expect this—unfortunately. My question was, "What was your most disap-pointing situation or event?"[15] Ben Sawatzky, founder of Spruceland Lumber, hesitated, and then in a quiet and measured tone, said, "My

---

[13]Paul Fast, quoted in *The Christian Entrepreneur*, 2:156-57.
[14]John Bunyan, *The Pilgrim's Progress* (Grand Rapids: Zondervan, 1967), p. 254.
[15]ELQ, question 20.

most disappointing situation was when I had been grooming a successor for myself for a number of years and he betrayed me. This was a personal betrayal by a close associate and friend."[16] The pain was still raw many years later. When another Entrepreneurial Leader, Volker Wagner, was interviewed, he responded likewise to that same question. He recounted his worst moment, twenty years later: "While Teldon [his company] was in soft receivership, a key executive betrayed my trust. This situation drove me to my knees before God."[17] In both cases the betrayers were fellow Christians, and in one case an elder of the church.

The vast majority of Entrepreneurial Leaders, though all financially successful and with a high dose of business acumen, suffered some sort of betrayal. The bottom line is that someone has done harm, economic or otherwise, to them that affected them and their company. This can undermine one's faith and confidence, especially when the other person is a Christian. Or should it? In an odd way, should we take the approach that it simply confirms the nature of people, that people are corrupt and sinful? The Old Testament talks of Cain and Abel. Jesus talks of wolves in sheep's clothing. Jesus, of course, was betrayed by one of his hand-picked disciples. Matthew talks about the need to be wary of untrustworthy people (Mt 10:17). Peter denied Christ three times. Paul speaks of being in danger from false believers (2 Cor 11:26).

Betrayal reminds us of the core sinfulness of people, that negative emotions or motivations can take root and overcome positive actions. Money is often at the heart of betrayal. Betrayal causes us to understand more fully the experience of Christ. Betrayal teaches us to stay on the high road and not to bring ourselves down to the level of the betrayers: forces of darkness and light. One key lesson for entrepreneurial leaders is to have a realistic view of human nature, and recognize that betrayal, even among close friends and associates, is always a realistic possibility. If betrayal occurs, there may be powerful lessons to be learned about yourself and your relations with others. It can be a time of sober self-reflection. But this can lead us to be both shrewd and innocent.

---

[16]Sawatzky, quoted in *Entrepreneurial Leaders*, 5:191.
[17]Volker Wagner, quoted in *Entrepreneurial Leaders*, 3:220.

Principle 4: Balancing the Serpent and the Dove

A common concern among entrepreneurial leaders, especially less-experienced and more naive ones, is how to balance their faith and yet be effective in business. Faith sometimes becomes a recipe for being too kind, too forgiving, too generous, too understanding—with the net result that the company cannot sustain that approach and the company collapses under its own munificence. But how can an entrepreneur maintain a balance?

We discussed the parable of the talents and the five-talent person who invested shrewdly in chapter six. In another parable in Luke 16 Jesus commends the "shrewd manager" and notes that "the people of this world are more shrewd in dealing with their own kind than are the people of the light" (Lk 16:8). But shrewdness is often associated with evil intent. Paul in Corinthians says we are not unaware of the devil's schemes (2 Cor 11:14-15). The truth is that all of us are a mixture. Those that have become Christians are new creatures. But they are not fully sanctified. Some of the old nature persists. Thus Thomas à Kempis in *The Imitation of Christ* contrasts faith in the Lord with faith in people. He refers to the fallen nature of people:

> In whom shall I put my faith, Lord? In whom but You? You are the truth which does not deceive and cannot be deceived. Every man, on the other hand, is a liar, weak, unstable, and likely to err, especially in words, so that one ought not to be too quick to believe even that which seems, on the face of it, to sound true.[18]

So, we are aware of the nature of evil, but how to deal with it? Jesus gives us an extraordinary answer.

"I am sending you out like sheep among wolves. Therefore be as shrewd as snakes and as innocent as doves" (Mt 10:16). This verse is an antidote to the naiveté of many Christians and may be among the most important for a Christian in business to fully understand. What is the meaning of "Be as shrewd as snakes"?

The disciples of Christ are hated and persecuted as *serpents*, and

---

[18]Thomas à Kempis, *Imitation of Christ*, trans. Aloysius Croft and Harold Bolton (Mineola, NY: Dover, 2003), p. 93

their ruin is sought; therefore they need the *serpent's* wisdom. Note, it is the will of Christ that his people and ministers, so exposed to troubles in this world, as they usually are, should not needlessly expose themselves but use all fair and lawful means for their own preservation. Christ gave us an example of this wisdom, . . . besides the many escapes he made out of the hands of his enemies, till his hour was come. See an instance of Paul's wisdom in Acts 23:6, Acts 26:7. . . . It is the wisdom of the serpent to secure his head, that it may not be broken, to stop his ear to the voice of the charmer (Ps 58:4, Ps 58:5), and to take shelter in the clefts of the rocks; and herein we may be wise as serpents. We must be wise, not to pull trouble upon our own heads; wise to keep silence in an evil time, and not to give offence, if we can help it.[19]

To be shrewd in business means using a calculated practical wisdom but not engaging in so-called sharp practice to gain unfair advantage. This is why Jesus adds the second half of the sentence: "Be as innocent as doves." We must use the harmlessness of the dove to bear injuries, rather than the subtlety of the serpent to offer or to return one. The challenge for entrepreneurial leaders is to be able to balance the serpent and the dove, and to be under no illusions as to human nature. When dishonest dealing does come, as it likely will, Paul Fast offers some wisdom: "You're going to get shafted in business. You'll get wronged somewhere along the way. I, personally, always tell myself to never harbor grudges, never harbor bitterness if something unjust happens to you. It's very difficult at times, but that's a principle we live by."[20] When we balance the serpent and the dove we may be successful but we may also fail. The next principle deals with this.

Principle 5: Handling Both Financial Rewards and Losses

How can we witness through the success or failure of our enterprise? Or should we even try? The Lord has "blessed" me, says one Entre-

---

[19]*Matthew Henry Commentary*, Bible Study Tools, www.biblestudytools.com/commentaries/matthew-henry-complete/matthew/10.html.
[20]Fast, quoted in *The Christian Entrepreneur*, p. 159.

preneurial Leader, meaning of course, full of financial rewards.[21] We have yet to hear someone say "I am dirt poor, almost destitute, and the Lord has blessed me." This is interesting because Jesus, who came to fulfill the law, does not equate blessing with financial abundance. In fact, Jesus says "blessed are you who are poor" (Lk 6:20). There are, however, many books that unashamedly advance some version of a prosperity theology in which a Christian life is intermeshed with financial abundance. One such book that promotes this message is the *Prayer of Jabez*, although perhaps not in the business sense.[22] If you say the prayer and follow God's ways, you will increase your property. It seems more of an offshoot of the prosperity gospel rather than a true Christian message.

While the intermeshing of following God and achieving financial success unite in an unholy matrimony in the prosperity theology, there have long been couplings between faith and financial well-being. The association of Protestantism and financial success was highlighted by German sociologist Max Weber.[23] Weber noted the association—far removed from prosperity theology—that certain Protestant groups achieved unusual financial success due to their faith-motivated hard work, thrift and wise stewardship. Modern-day Protestantism has retained some of the emphasis on hard work, but thrift and wise stewardship have been drowned in a sea of engulfing consumerist culture.

A statement posed to Entrepreneurial Leaders was, "I believe God blesses business people in proportion to the degree they follow a Christian approach to life."[24] The issue behind this question was identified by Max Weber. He noted that ascetic Protestants received "the comforting assurance that the unequal distribution of the goods of this world was a special dispensation of Divine Providence."[25]

---

[21]See also our discussion of the meaning of "blessing" in chap. 6.

[22]Bruce Wilkinson, *The Prayer of Jabez: Breaking Through to the Blessed Life* (Sisters, OR: Multnomah, 2000).

[23]See the exposition of this in the chapter "Creativity" in R. Paul Stevens, *Doing God's Business* (Grand Rapids: Eerdmans, 2006), pp. 164-83.

[24]ELQ, section D, question 20.

[25]Max Weber, *The Protestant Ethic and the Spirit of Capitalism*, trans. Talcott Parsons (New York: Charles Scribner's, 1958), p. 177.

This poses an interesting question, with answers varying depending on the theological framework of the particular entrepreneurial leader. Put simply, does God bless a person financially to the extent he or she is true to the faith? Often entrepreneurs will say that God has blessed them financially and that they attribute it to their Christian conviction. But what about an entrepreneur who is very faithful and yet hasn't achieved financial success?

Is it a perversion of the gospel to imply the blessings of the Lord are primarily financial? Is that the end game? This seems to be an underlying assumption among some entrepreneurs. The challenge for entrepreneurs is that things don't always work out. In fact, all studies show that businesses fail more often than they succeed. This is the nature of the process. Few ventures succeed on a grand scale, and many die a quiet death. Failure is especially part of the experience of entrepreneurs as they are operating on the edge, outside the box, treading in new territory and thus with a great chance to fail.

One notable example of achieving the heights of success and then a large-scale failure is the story of Loewen Funeral Homes. Ray Loewen was at one time a billionaire and ranked as the eighteenth wealthiest person in Canada. From 1967 to 1999 the Loewen Group's reputation in the funeral home industry grew rapidly throughout North America, and the company was recognized as a leading industry consolidator in the 1990s. Ray Loewen explains that

> Our earnings had compounded for 8 years at 30% on a fully-diluted basis—and our stock had gone up 20 fold. The Loewen Group had truly become a darling North American growth story. By 1998 we had approximately $3 billion in revenue and 16,000 employees. We also had a market capitalization of $2 billion and were listed on both the New York and NASDAQ stock exchanges in the US, as well as the Toronto and Montreal stock exchanges in Canada.[26]

Loewen was basking in the glow of success. He had visions of pursuing great philanthropic projects in the near future. There was no inkling of what was to come.

---

[26]Ray Loewen, quoted in *The Christian Entrepreneur*, 2:237-38.

The Loewen Group was sued by a disgruntled funeral home operator in the southern United States. The claim against them was in the millions, but when the judgment was rendered against the Loewen Group in 1995, an enormous amount was included by way of punitive damages. Ray Loewen recalls vividly,

> My worst moment was sitting in a Jackson, Mississippi, court room and hearing a $500 million judgment against The Loewen Group. This meant we had to post a bond of $625 million. Our book value was not even that large at the time even though our market capitalization was about $2 billion. I instinctively knew that our growth story was finished, barring a miracle.[27]

No miracle came. This spectacular collapse was well-documented in North American media at the time and for years thereafter. Ray Loewen believed that there were individuals who could have assisted in mitigating the fallout from this occurrence, but when momentum shifted, key management began to look for other opportunities, rather than digging in deeper.

The lessons learned by entrepreneurial leaders can minister to and encourage others struggling with similar issues. Ray Loewen, now removed by many years from those cataclysmic events, could reflect and say, "I have tried very hard to be a forgiving person. I have taken literally the Bible's admonition that vengeance belongs to God. I have taken seriously that God is faithful in good times and has purposes in bad times."[28] He cited two passages as particularly meaningful. The first is Job 30:20-21:

> I cry out to you, God, but you do not answer;
>   I stand up, but you merely look at me.
> You turn on me ruthlessly;
>   with the might of your hand you attack me.

The second is 1 Peter 1:6-7:

> In all this you greatly rejoice, though now for a little while you may

---

[27]Ibid., p. 241.
[28]Ibid., p. 244.

have had to suffer grief in all kinds of trials. These have come so that your faith—of greater worth than gold, which perishes even though refined by fire—may be proved genuine and may result in praise, glory and honor when Jesus Christ is revealed.

Few people could apply those passages so deeply.

Related to the issue of financial success is the principle of giving.

Principle 6: Giving Effectively

Another aspect of sustaining entrepreneurial leadership is to learn to give effectively. Entrepreneurs usually don't start off as wealthy, and they often are quite parsimonious as they build their business. Giving can be challenging during the lean years. There are unique financial dynamics for entrepreneurs compared to salaried individuals. Most members of a church know their monthly income; they receive a pay stub which confirms it. Not so for entrepreneurs. They may have no income or inconsistent income. We ask tongue-in-cheek whether they should take money out of the offering plate if they are losing money that month? Further, they may be taking out a minimum amount of money from a company with the expectation of a greater future return when the business is sold. Entrepreneurs may need to keep funds in the company as a contingency reserve. The situation becomes very different for entrepreneurs once they have achieved financial success.

One of the privileges of my (Rick's) position with a wealth management firm is that with an entire team I am able to advise financially successful Christian entrepreneurs regarding their giving strategies. But financially successful entrepreneurs typically remember the lean years, and thus they strive to give money away wisely. There is no shortage of worthy options. But a set of principles must be established. At the firm where I work, we are part of the Kingdom Advisors Network, which provides teaching materials on good stewardship from Ronald Blue & Co.[29] A recognition by entrepreneurs that they are stewards of resources for the furtherance of kingdom work is a great ministry opportunity.

---

[29]See Kingdom Advisors Network's website at www.kingdomadvisors.org.

There are five aspects of entrepreneurial giving. First, research literature reveals that successful entrepreneurs are exceptionally generous.[30] Many universities would be sorely underfunded if not for the generosity of entrepreneurs. Second, entrepreneurs are often active philanthropists; they want to know firsthand what results are being achieved. One example is Ben Sawatzky. He explains that

> My wife and I take a period of time away from distractions in order to consider all funding requests. We have four children and they're all on the board of directors of the foundation now. We take a whole family weekend in order to study requests and to get some questions answered. We spend time in both private and corporate prayer over these requests and we make our gifting decisions.[31]

Third, they are very results oriented. They want to know about outcomes. Fourth, they want to know about the business model of the organization they are supporting. Is their contribution a stopgap measure or is it a means of launching a self-sustaining enterprise? Last, entrepreneurs, like most donors, do not want to reward inefficiency and cover up past mistakes. Rod Bergen, secretary of Jim Pattison Foundation, which has distributed approximately $400 million over the years, wants to support those with a track record of success rather than failure.

The act of giving, which is part of worship, could also be included as part of Principle 4, "Engaging in Spiritual Disciplines," in chapter eight. As Carl Kreider notes, "There is a leanness of soul that comes from a failure to give each week as an act of worship."[32] On the other side, those who give generously gain spiritual satisfaction. One Entrepreneurial Leader comments that "Because God has given me a lot, I have to be a stronger steward and take care of my resources.

---

[30]Most leading entrepreneurship textbooks recount the generosity of entrepreneurial philanthropists. See, for example, Jeffry A. Timmons and Stephen Spinelli, *New Venture Creation: Entrepreneurship for the 21st Century*, 7th ed. (New York: McGraw-Hill/Irwin, 2007), and Robert Hisrich, Michael Peters and Dean Shepherd, *Entrepreneurship: Theory, Process and Practice*, 9th ed. (New York: McGraw-Hill/Irwin, 2013).

[31]Sawatzky, quoted in *Entrepreneurial Leaders,* pp. 194-95.

[32]Carl Kreider, *The Christian Entrepreneur* (Waterloo, ON: Herald Press, 1980), p. 161.

It's one of the strong principles of which all people should know: the more you give the more you get back. That's simple faith. You can call it crazy, but that's what it is."[33] Another Entrepreneurial Leader explains it this way: "With privilege also comes huge responsibility. . . . We are responsible for helping organizations, churches, conferences and missions. We are called to write the bigger cheques. I have no problems with that. . . . I call that a responsibility, but I would also call it a privilege."[34] One Entrepreneurial Leader concurred with the value of the giving process: "Watch out for greed! The best way to overcome greed is to write big checks and give money away. It is liberating!"[35] Entrepreneurial leaders recognize that giving is not a burden but an opportunity. But our stewardship responsibilities include not only what we do with our money but how we spend our time.

Principle 7: Managing the Work-Life Tension

Unquestionably the number one issue faced by people in challenging occupations is work-life balance. Proper management of work-life tension will facilitate ministry to relationships within the workplace and with family and friends outside of it. Bored, entrepreneurs are not. But that very dynamic of "can't wait to get to work" and the total engagement needed to implement a new enterprise often means that families are neglected, personal recreation time is missed, ongoing and lifelong learning is short-circuited. Entrepreneurs will frequently cut a check rather than show up for meetings. Entrepreneurs are pursuing their passion—play and work all rolled into one. But there is a particular problem with that.

Some entrepreneurs say they cannot give quantity time to their children and spouse, so they claim to give quality time, concentrated doses of personal engagement to impact another's life. But the reality is that quality time cannot be organized. It is something that "happens" in the context of quantity time. In the Bible the two Greek

---

[33]Allan Skidmore, quoted in *Entrepreneurial Leaders*, 5:213-14.
[34]Peter Niebuhr, quoted in ibid., 1:215.
[35]Wagner, quoted in ibid., p. 224.

words for this are first, *chronos*, from which we get the English word *chronological*. This is clock time, calendar time, the kind of time that can be organized through a time management seminar. But the other Greek word for time in the Bible is *kairos*. This is special time, quality time, time that is fraught with consequences, the time of repentance or renewal. Martin Luther said the Word of God is like a thunderstorm that comes over a city. This is their *kairos*. If they respond, they will be healed and renewed. But if they do not respond, the storm moves on. So when Scripture says to "mak[e] the most of every opportunity" (Eph 5:16), it is not merely saying "organize your time for maximum effectiveness"—never, of course, a bad thing to do—but it means to discern what time it is. That seems to be one of the messages of Ecclesiastes. There is a time for everything, says the Professor in that Old Testament book (not time to do everything), but this is not a meaningless round. There are seasons in time, times of more intensive engagement in one activity and then time to do something different. But there is even more. God has built eternity into time, and we have to not only be stewards of time but discern when *chronos* moves to *kairos*. It happens in a family when a son or daughter asks a profound question, often at the worst possible moment, or when an employee hits us with something at the most inconvenient moment, or when our spouse needs to share something deep and personal just as we are leaving for an important meeting. Time is not our enemy, not a scarce resource. We have all the time we need, all the time God gives us to do what God wants in a given day. Often, time is a more precious resource than money.

The seven principles discussed in this chapter provide ways to overcome the challenges of the marketplace and to not only sustain Christian entrepreneurial leadership but to use it as a basis for ministry. We have tried to build a foundation through the chapters of this book, moving from a clear understanding of entrepreneurial leadership through to core concepts and then practicing and sustaining it. This process has provided a foundation to address how entrepreneurial leaders can make a difference.

For Reflection and Discussion

1. Choose one of the themes of this chapter that challenged you. Share it with someone else, possibly a colleague or a spouse. Do you want to grow in this area? Can you ask someone to hold you accountable in this area of your life?

2. This chapter has explored some of the challenges of the ministry of entrepreneurship. But we have also considered entrepreneurship as a ministry, a way of serving God, people and creation. Consider your own work, or the work of a colleague or friend. In what ways do you see this as a ministry?

Mini Bible Study. Read Luke's version of the beatitudes (the blessings) in Luke 6:17-36. Which of the "blessings" have you experienced? Which statements deeply trouble you? Why?

10

Making a Difference

*The business life appears as an extremely demanding
vocation, making great claims on the believer's character
and calling for a close, humble, faithful, hopeful, and
self-distrustful walk with God. Prayer, honest fellowship
with other Christians in accountability relationships of full
frankness, and constant reflection before God on what is
best, according to the Bible standards of righteousness,
love, and wisdom, are necessities. . . . Character counts no
less than skills and technical know-how if one is to glorify
God in business life.*

J. I. PACKER,
"THE CHRISTIAN'S PURPOSE IN BUSINESS"

The unique aspects of Christian entrepreneurial leadership have
been explored throughout this book: soul and spirituality, meaning
and work ethic, risk and reward, finding your calling, and practicing
and sustaining entrepreneurial leadership. A proper handling of
these issues develops and reflects character, which, as Packer notes
in the epigraph, is at the core of Christ-directed behavior. In this
final chapter we want to build on this foundation of well-rounded
character to explore how and where to deploy entrepreneurial
leadership to make a difference and how to maintain this in the
long run.

Making a Difference in Church

Let's start with what should be every entrepreneur's spiritual backyard—the church. How can entrepreneurs make a difference in church? We wish this were an easy subject to explore, but it is not. The relationship between entrepreneurs and the church is often characterized by alienation, disillusionment and disappointment. The Entrepreneurial Leader Research Program concluded that Entrepreneurial Leaders were, in many cases, disconnected from the church they attended. Why? The ELRP indicates that entrepreneurs are often not affirmed in their churches and are not confident in the ability of church leadership to address business-related issues. Entrepreneurs often do not find their churches open to new ideas or willing to make changes. They feel that whatever gifts they may have for business do not seem to be of use in the church. Further the church does not usually affirm that what they are doing is full-time ministry in the world, although they should as explained earlier. Of course that is true for many besides pastors, missionaries and major church volunteers. This lack of connection between entrepreneurial leaders and their churches, unfortunately, deprives both of synergistic benefits.

Here is the nub of the matter. On one hand entrepreneurs seem not to find the church to be an important part of their vocational and spiritual formation, except in some rare cases. They may simply not be involved. On the other hand the church does not seem to prioritize supporting and equipping entrepreneurs for their ministry in the workplace. There are pockets of great support by churches of entrepreneurs, but these are typically unique circumstances. Sometimes the pastor may have a business background, some past eye-opening experience or significant exposure to the marketplace, and thus the church leader is more attuned to the possibilities of engaging entrepreneurs within the church.[1] Overall, there appears to be a great opportunity wasted to fully engage Christian entrepreneurial leaders in the church community.[2] While reviewing a twenty-

---

[1]For a comprehensive survey see C. Neal Johnson, *Business as Mission: A Comprehensive Guide to Theory and Practice* (Downers Gove, IL: InterVarsity Press, 2009).
[2]Principle 6, "Seeking Wise Counsel," in chap. 8 noted the opportunity for church lead-

eight-page booklet published in the United Kingdom under the title of *The Entrepreneur and the Church*, I (Rick) discovered that its author, Bill Bolton, an experienced entrepreneurship consultant, had reached a similar finding in the UK context.[3] Bolton concluded that "Releasing the entrepreneurial talent among God's people is the greatest task facing the church today. It is the Entrepreneurial Imperative."[4] Let's consider first of all the entrepreneur's attitude toward the church.

1. Why entrepreneurs struggle in their relationship with the church. Entrepreneurial Leaders were asked to respond (scale of strongly disagree [1] to strongly agree [10]) to the following question: "I have discovered my calling in business and have integrated it with my faith largely *through my own efforts*."[5] Interestingly, 68 percent of respondents scored 8-10. Entrepreneurial Leaders have pursued this issue with very little input from others. We conclude that most Entrepreneurial Leaders are often engaged in a lonely, individual quest to apply their calling usually without help from the church.

Entrepreneurial Leaders were asked whether anyone affirmed their calling.[6] The ELRP revealed that the church has played an insignificant role in affirming the calling of Entrepreneurial Leaders.[7] In terms of priority, Entrepreneurial Leaders first receive affirmation from immediate family, often a spouse. The next most common response in order of frequency was that affirmation is *not* received from anyone. Affirmation from a friend is cited, and then affirmation is received from a business contact. Only as a fifth source of affirmation is church listed. Entrepreneurial Leaders occasionally cited a pastor who affirmed their calling. But let's now look at the other side of the problem, the church's relation with entrepreneurs. Part of the problem is that church leaders

---

ers to offer support to entrepreneurial leaders.

[3]Bill Bolton, *The Entrepreneur and the Church* (Cambridge, UK: Grove Books, 2006), p. 4.

[4]See my review of this book: Richard J. Goossen, *Faith in Business Quarterly* 11, no. 2 (2007): 19-22.

[5]ELQ, section D, question 5. See ELRP Analysis.

[6]ELQ, question 20. See ELRP Analysis.

[7]By *church* I mean the leadership, such as pastoral staff, of the congregation where the Entrepreneurial Leaders are members or attend regularly.

often do not think that what entrepreneurs are doing in the world is important, is part of kingdom ministry or is doing "God's work." I (Rick) found this out at a seminary conference marketed to pastors, where I was speaking on "Business as Mission." The conference began with an embarrassing and telltale moment. The keynote speaker started by innocently asking, "Can I see by a show of hands the pastors and church workers who are here?" At first no hands were raised; then, slowly and cautiously, two pairs of hands went up out of a group of forty attendees. The clear message: business people thought this topic was important; church leadership did not.

Entrepreneurial Leaders feel strongly called to entrepreneurship, and yet they feel that their own church leadership does not offer support in affirming their calling or even understanding their motivations. While church leaders may view entrepreneurs as a source of financial support, the feeling is not mutual. Entrepreneurial Leaders do not view themselves as merely being sources of financing for other mission ventures but also wish to apply a range of their skills and creativity. Along with an entrepreneur's wallet comes his entrepreneurial spirit. As a result, entrepreneurs often become disenchanted. In some instances there may be some open criticism of business people and entrepreneurs, which leads from disenchantment to disenfranchisement. One Catholic writer, Robert A. Sirico, argues that many business people have stopped actively participating in their religious communities because of hostility toward free enterprise by ministers and priests.[8] One can only speculate at how many entrepreneurs have lost an active faith. Let's look more closely at how entrepreneurs relate to the church.

The ELRP reveals four types of responses of Entrepreneurial Leaders in relation to the church. First, they may simply disengage; they remove themselves from the church community entirely. Second, they remain in the church but are passive. They sit in a comfortable pew through sheer inertia, but have checked their mind out long ago. Third, they remain in the church and are active in their faith, but realize that the most efficient and effective use of their gifts is through a parachurch

---

[8]Robert A. Sirico, "A Worthy Calling," *Acton Institute*, November 22, 1993, www.acton
.org/public-policy/business-society/entrepreneurial-voc/worthy-calling.

organization; they bypass their home church almost entirely. Last, they remain and are active in the church; they may have a pastor who is particularly adept at working with the business community or they may simply be committed to working through the challenges. While we do not wish to quibble over the percentages in each category, we can conclude that a significant portion of the entrepreneurial talent of people sitting in the very pews of the church is withering on the vine.

2. Why the church struggles with entrepreneurs. Let's be frank: entrepreneurs are not always the easiest people to deal with. In fact, entrepreneurs may be among the most challenging for any organization. They can be impatient, action-oriented and nonbureaucratic. How can the church work to mobilize all the entrepreneurs in its midst to greater effectiveness? There is a talented and dynamic group of people within the church's circle that views its workplace as a mission field. These talents can help the church as well as the workplace. The challenge for the church is to harness, rather than squelch, the energies and passions of entrepreneurs in their midst. Entrepreneurs generally think big. I (Rick) heard Bill Bright, founder of Campus Crusade for Christ, comment years ago at a conference that "Small plans do not inflame the minds of men." We could add, particularly with entrepreneurs. One Entrepreneurial Leader explained his early ambition:

> I wanted to change the world by going into business rather than the Church. My family thought that because I was "religious," it was logical that I should become a full-time paid vicar. Also, I was pressurized by churchmen to become a vicar. My expression at the time was that I wanted to blow up our society from within, rather than make minor explosions on the fringe.[9]

Back in 1980 Carl Kreider, in *The Christian Entrepreneur*, identified the contribution of the entrepreneur: "The unique skills they [Christian entrepreneurs] have gained in their experience in their private businesses can and should be used to serve the larger cause of the church operating through its institutions."[10] The dissatis-

---

[9]John Lovatt, quoted in *Entrepreneurial Leaders: Reflections on Faith and Work*, ed. Richard J. Goossen (Langley, BC: Trinity Western University, 2007–2010), 4:207.
[10]Carl Kreider, *The Christian Entrepreneur* (Waterloo, ON: Herald Press, 1980), p. 197.

faction of entrepreneurs with the church will have an enormous impact that will not be felt for another generation—but the impact can either be the revitalization and renewal of the faith or an irreparable slide into irrelevancy. Are Christian institutions characterized by being innovative, creative, forward-thinking? Or are they stagnant, lifeless, with no new ideas and no vitality?

Pastors, when involved in an active relationship with an entrepreneur, can have a life-changing impact. These are refreshing exceptions. One Entrepreneurial Leader explained that "My pastor definitely encouraged me in my calling. He believed that I could glorify God in the business realm every bit as much as a person called to ministry within the church. He viewed the kingdom of God as extending into all realms including the business realm."[11] The implications of this fact are enormous for both entrepreneurial leaders and the church.

3. Bridging the entrepreneur–church gap. There is clearly a communication gap between most entrepreneurs and their churches. How can this be bridged? To start with, what do entrepreneurs want? Do they want preferential treatment? No! The ELRP reveals that their requests are quite sensible and modest. First, entrepreneurs long to have their calling validated. They don't want a pedestal; they just want an equal place at the table. Second, they want prayer and encouragement—not at the expense of others, though. They are just saying that they value prayer and encouragement from the church leaders they respect—that means a lot to them. Third, they want church leadership to understand and respect them. They often don't feel the love from the pulpit. A business person may either be an explicit whipping boy or the pastor may adopt outmoded zero-sum game thinking of the money-grubbing entrepreneur who only benefits at the expense of others. Fourth, Entrepreneurial Leaders want solid biblical teaching. They pursue excellence and they recognize that in others. No more and no less, and not an entrepreneur-specific sermon—just give them good biblical insight.

---

[11]Ken Ewert, quoted in *The Christian Entrepreneur: Insights from the Marketplace*, ed. Richard J. Goossen (Langley, BC: Trinity Western University, 2005–2006), 1:102.

What are some practical action steps for a church? There are four ways for a church to build good relations with entrepreneurs in their midst. First, a church leader should visit entrepreneurs at their place of business. This simple action will not only convey respect and appreciation, but it will also allow a pastor to understand more intimately the entrepreneur's daily environment. Second, understand the whole person of an entrepreneur. Don't view an entrepreneur as a walking wallet. Instead, understand the entrepreneur's spiritual dimensions also. Third, create a culture that welcomes entrepreneurs. This can be done by being open to considering new ideas; don't say "we've never done it that way before" with the implication that we never will. Fourth, become a place where all members can utilize their gifts, exercise their calling, within a community of fellowship. Discover the gifts and resources of the entrepreneur and put them to use. The church can greatly help its own cause by tapping into the tremendous resources within its midst—it doesn't have to go outside its walls to find these people. We earlier noted the importance of support networks for entrepreneurs; church leaders can play a pivotal role "during the difficult and lonely times that occur throughout the entrepreneurial process."[12]

As a further resource, in *The Equipper's Guide to Every-Member Ministry* I (Paul) offer several practical steps churches can take in equipping business and professional people. They include teaching a theology of work, interviewing marketplace ministers in the worship service, offering intercessory prayers for members in the marketplace, commissioning marketplace ministers, offering integrative courses in the adult education program, and facilitating networking of people engaged in similar marketplace involvements.[13]

We have pointed out what the church can do, but what about entrepreneurs? The following are four practices for entrepreneurs to

---

[12]Robert Hisrich, Michael Peters and Dean Shepherd, *Entrepreneurship: Theory, Process and Practice*, 9th ed. (New York: McGraw-Hill/Irwin, 2013), p. 20.

[13]R. Paul Stevens, *The Equipper's Guide to Every-Member Ministry* (Vancouver: Regent College Publishing, 2000), pp. 91-112.

work with churches more effectively. First, they should focus on providing their "transferable skills" from the marketplace. They may be resourceful and creative. They may have legal, accounting and other technical skills. They may have leadership skills that can be put to good use in a home study group. The entrepreneur should take the initiative to offer their talents for the benefit of the church. Second, entrepreneurs need to recognize that commercial success does not and should not translate to spiritual influence. They may be very wealthy—but they may also be immature in their faith. A $100 million net worth doesn't mean the entrepreneur should be chairperson of the building committee and on the board of elders. Third, entrepreneurs can focus on collaboration. They are in an environment that needs to respect the opinion of the entire congregation. They are not in a lone-ranger environment single-handedly overcoming the odds. Fourth, entrepreneurs should be discreet but not invisible. Some entrepreneurs don't want attention (the opposite extreme of using wealth to buy influence). The danger is that discreteness may become detachment. Entrepreneurs need to get involved. In short, both entrepreneurs and church leaders can engage in a number of simple practices as a pathway to begin more fruitful collaboration for the benefit of kingdom-building activities.

When committed entrepreneurs realize that operating within the church will not only be frustrating for them but for their church leaders, they sometimes exercise their gifts in a positive way—but within parachurch organizations. To that we now turn.

Making a Difference in Denominations and Parachurch Organizations

The ELRP indicates that the chief beneficiaries of the energy of Entrepreneurial Leaders are often parachurch organizations. Many of these organizations have a preponderance of entrepreneurs in leadership positions. Entrepreneurial Leaders were asked, "Have you been involved in para-church organizations and how?"[14] For

---

[14]ELQ, question 35.

those who were involved, 80 percent of their participation was either on the board or they contributed financially to parachurch organizations; only a very small number (approximately 5 percent) were not involved in any way.[15] Entrepreneurs are doers, they get involved, and they want to make a difference. The only question is where this entrepreneurial energy will be directed. When they are not involved in church leadership, they often take on leadership in parachurch organizations.

The ELRP asked, "Have you been involved in your church denomination and how?"[16] One-third of respondents were not involved in any way with their denomination, while one-quarter were involved in some form of leadership.[17] This response is not surprising in many ways. Entrepreneurs are action-oriented doers; they are not typically interested in getting involved in committees and deliberations. Most entrepreneurial companies are characterized by very flat organizational structures; to most entrepreneurs any form of hierarchy is anathema.[18] As a result, many entrepreneurs do not pursue opportunities to sit on a denominational board. While the majority of Entrepreneurial Leaders are reflected in the previous summary, others recognized the value of institutional involvement. One Entrepreneurial Leader commented, "I have been active in [my denomination] at the local, national and provincial levels. My participation on various boards has enriched my appreciation for church institutions. I have benefited from the friendships and spiritual guidance."[19]

Parachurch organizations that are particularly vexing to entrepreneurs are Christian educational institutions. Entrepreneurial Leaders are often connected to the business program of a Christian education institution due to clear synergies. Entrepre-

---

[15]See ELRP Analysis.

[16]ELQ, question 34.

[17]See ELRP Analysis.

[18]See chap. 6, "Henry Mintzberg: Entrepreneurship and Organizations," in *Entrepreneurial Excellence*, ed. Richard J. Goossen (Franklin Lakes, NJ: Career Press, 2007), pp. 111-20.

[19]Arthur Block, quoted in *The Christian Entrepreneur*, 1:53.

neurs can offer mentoring to individual students and presentations to groups, and they are often a source of financial contributions. Meanwhile, an educational institution can provide
competent students for the entrepreneur's business and bring in
renowned guest lecturers for high-level inspiration. Despite the
lure of a symbiotic relationship, potential is often not realized.
The centuries-old mode of delivering university education, reflected even in institutions formed within recent times, provides
a culture clash with entrepreneurs. The problem and core challenge is that leaders of educational institutions react slowly to
change; by contrast, entrepreneurial leaders embrace change. A
case in point is the advent of rapid technological advances in how
education content can be delivered. For example, education no
longer needs to be delivered in a single physical location. Instead,
the institutions that are thriving have recognized that education
can be delivered through various blended online models. This approach is much more attractive to the ongoing midcareer learner
who cannot take one to three years off for a degree. The institutions that have benefitted extraordinarily from the technological
changes have been new or recently reinvigorated institutions,
such as the University of Phoenix and, in a Christian context,
Grand Canyon University and Bakke Graduate University. In
short, Christian entrepreneurial leaders are prone to support institutions that reflect their own values. They will look for innovative institutions. Sadly, many Christian educational institutions do not adapt rapidly to changing environments and this
undermines their long-term sustainability. Beyond alumni and
friends of an institution, the broader Christian community will
also be detrimentally affected. The institution will no longer be
able to transmit knowledge from one generation of leaders to the
next. The issue of Christian educational institutions relates to the
question of legacy on an institutional level. But what about legacy
at a personal level? What are we personally doing to make a difference beyond our own lifespan?

Making a Difference for Future Generations

Legacy is based in lessons and knowledge that are transmitted from one generation to the next. John C. Maxwell refers to the "Law of Legacy," which states "True success is measured by succession."[20] Legacy building is part of the biblical mandate. The dissemination of entrepreneurial wisdom from within the Christian community is a vital part of fostering a spiritual legacy. The Bible highlights the importance of ongoing regeneration among believers.[21] In the New Testament, Paul exhorts Timothy to "entrust [the things you have heard me say] to reliable people who will also be qualified to teach others" (2 Tim 2:2). In another instance Paul refers to the passing on of a legacy: "So then, brothers and sisters, stand firm and hold fast to the teachings we passed on to you, whether by word of mouth or by letter" (2 Thess 2:15). Christian leaders of the present generation likewise recognize the significance of this biblical truth. Rick Warren, for example, in *The Purpose-Driven Life* talks about passing on what you know to others.[22]

Christians should embody a clear focus and purpose. We are instructed, "let us throw off everything that hinders and the sin that so easily entangles. And let us run with perseverance the race marked out for us" (Heb 12:1). There are important lessons here: get rid of the unimportant, get rid of the sin which ensnares and entraps, with endurance be trained and equipped, then *run*. Rather than a job, this is a race in a competition with a finish line and an audience. Philippians speaks of pressing on toward the goal (Phil 3:12-14). But can we keep doing it with integrity until the conclusion of the race?

---

[20] John C. Maxwell, introduction to *The Maxwell Leadership Bible* (Nashville: Thomas Nelson, 2002).

[21] Some commentators may refer to this concept of spiritual legacy as "spiritual capital." *Spiritual capital* can be defined as "the fund of beliefs, examples and commitments that are transmitted from generation to generation through a religious tradition, and which attach people to the transcendental source of human happiness" (Theodore Roosevelt Malloch, *Spiritual Enterprise: Doing Virtuous Business* [New York: Encounter Books, 2008], pp. 11-12). For a review of Malloch's book on this topic see Richard J. Goossen, "Book Review of *Spiritual Enterprise: Doing Virtuous Business*," *Faith in Business Quarterly* 12, no. 3 (2009): 9-10.

[22] Rick Warren, *The Purpose-Driven Life* (Grand Rapids: Zondervan, 2002), pp. 309-10.

Making a Difference to the End

We now turn to making a difference—wherever and however—for the long haul. The reality is that many do not end well and we must find out why and what to do about it.

1. An example of not finishing well. The story of King Solomon in the Kings section of the Old Testament provides an important lesson for entrepreneurs. After reciting all the wonderful things Solomon did, his achievements, projects and wisdom, the narrator uses the word *however.* "King Solomon, however, loved many foreign women. . . . Solomon held fast to them in love." In fact he had a lot of wives to hold fast to, seven hundred wives and three hundred concubines. Did he know all their names? "As Solomon grew old," continues the narrator, "his wives turned his heart after other gods, and his heart was not fully devoted to the LORD his God, as the heart of David his father had been" (1 Kings: 11:1-2, 4). Would that this only happened in Old Testament times!

Sometimes entrepreneurs become very successful and begin to amass fortunes, multiple houses, numerous and very expensive luxury cars, fabulous and very costly vacations, and their central love for Jesus and his kingdom grows cold. They may continue to show up to church services, but the passion for God has gone. They give into consumerism, into having the latest, into impressing people with their status-oriented lifestyle. And all too often their single-minded love for the wife of their youth is compromised, or they simply abandon their aging wife for a "new and younger model." Solomon did not finish well. He finished as a compromised old man with a dirty mind, as is so clearly revealed in another Old Testament book, the Song of Songs.[23] How did it happen for Solomon? We have much to learn negatively from him. It happened in stages, not all at once,

---

[23]This is not the place to expound the enigmatic book Song of Songs (Song of Solomon), but the best interpretation is that Solomon is in the process of acquiring yet one more beautiful young woman for his collection in the harem. She, however, is already pledged to a shepherd lover to whom she goes either in dream or reality. Meanwhile Solomon "courts" her by reciting her anatomical advantages while the shepherd lover, in the end, says something like, "Solomon can have his harem, but she is my one and only." It is a poem of the beauty of erotic love with covenant partners and disgust of Solomon's lust.

which is why even young entrepreneurs need to plan to finish well.

First Solomon used people as tools for his own projects. He oppressed the people. He wanted to build a fabulous temple, a gorgeous palace and then a palace for his wives, followed by store cities and special cities even for his horses and chariots. To do all this he had to squeeze all he could out of the people of Israel to fund and staff his grandiose projects. It was so bad that after he died the labor task master went to the work site and the laborers killed him. But there was more.

Solomon allowed himself to become sexually and sensually focused. This was probably happening as his male capacity for sexual arousal began to wane. So how does he deal with it? He takes on young and beautiful women to satisfy his sexual appetite. More and more of them in fact, even hundreds. But behind this was an even more subtle factor in Solomon's demise.

Solomon allowed his foreign wives to draw him away from single-minded devotion to the God of Israel. To accommodate his new sexual playmates he allowed them to continue their worship of various pagan gods, even to build temples and images to these vile gods, some of whom required sacrificing babies into the fiery flames while the drums beat so loudly that they drowned out the cries. Simply, Solomon became a universalist. He embraced religious pluralism. He did what is actually encouraged by many contemporary books and spokespersons. He moved from an exclusive faith to a universal faith, namely, that there is truth in all religions and we do not need to belong exclusively to one faith.

We can see that in many Christians who start well but all kinds of factors lead them to abandon that single-mindedness: how their own children have turned out, some good and some not so good; the influence of a pluralistic society; and often the influence of close associates in business from other religious backgrounds. And sometimes they marry a second or third time outside their faith and get sucked into something other than loving the Lord God with all their heart, soul, strength and mind. So much for Solomon. Even the centuries of raving about his wisdom cannot undo the fact that he did not finish well. But what about ourselves? Will we give in to one of the three big bugaboos that keep leaders from finishing well: sex, money or power?

2. A strategy for finishing well. A great beginning does not necessarily mean a great ending. And to finish well one has to practice what Eugene Peterson calls "a long obedience in the same direction" by maintaining goals and personal mission, pruning our lives of influences that would woo us away from God and his kingdom, and keeping in front of us all the way through what we are about in our lives and work. How do we finish strong? The apostle Paul has provided an inspiring epitaph: "I have fought the good fight, I have finished the race, I have kept the faith" (2 Tim 4:7). How do we push on purposefully to the end?

First, we must keep articulating our life goals, not just when we are young and are starting a new project, but all the way along. It is helpful to have a personal mission statement and to keep it before your eyes. Mine (Paul's) is to love God with all my heart; to love and cherish my wife and children through provision, affirmation and protection; to empower the people of God for service in the world and church; and to beautify God's world by making beautiful things. Dr. Walter Wright asks three questions: (1) What is the most important thing in your life right now (and do not quickly say "God")? (2) What do you want your life to be about? (3) At this point in your life what do you want to learn next?

Second, constantly refresh your sense of calling. We have highlighted the importance of finding your calling in chapter seven, throughout the text and in the subtitle of this book. Calling helps us finish well with respect to three of life's challenges. (1) It keeps us journeying purposefully to the very end of our lives.[24] (2) Calling helps to prevent us from confusing the termination of our occupations with the termination of our vocations—read "occupations"—the two are not the same.[25] (3) Calling encourages us to leave the entire

---

[24]Os Guinness, *The Call: Finding and Fulfilling the Central Purpose of Your Life* (Nashville: Word, 1998), pp. 241-42.
[25]Ibid., p. 242.

outcome of our lives to God. In one of the evocative Servant Songs in the Old Testament book of Isaiah, the Servant of the Lord says,

I have labored in vain;
    I have spent my strength for nothing at all.
Yet what is due me is in the LORD's hand,
    and my reward is with my God. (Is 49:4)

Third, each of us needs to have an accountability group. This is a small group of people who know us well and who are willing to meet with us from time to time to examine what we are doing with our lives, with our thoughts, with our talents and even with our money. They need to ask about our relationships, especially with spouse, children and people of the other sex. They need to explore our vulnerabilities and our strengths, and to name the lie in us. Yes, it is worth having an accountability group that may ask how much money we are making and what we are doing with it. David Hataj was one of my (Paul's) marketplace students at Regent College. Upon graduation he took over his father's precision-and-custom gear business. With entrepreneurial skill he grew from a small shop in Wisconsin to a major business that does custom gear manufacturing for printing presses and food-making machines, just to name a couple of applications. Their service is so good that David's shop operates at full capacity even though he does not spend a dollar on advertising. Recently he even posted on his website that he cannot take on any new customers for the time being. His earnings have skyrocketed from this and two other businesses he has started. But David and his wife, Tracy, decided at the very beginning to peg their income and lifestyle to a certain dollar amount. And they continue to live that way eighteen years after taking over the business, thus freeing up a large amount of money for reinvestment in the business and many wonderful projects that David has developed in needier parts of the world.

A good example in Scripture and a counterpoise to Solomon is Samuel, the leader of Israel during the time of the judges. He was able to finish well. His last speech is a wonderful summary of his life.

"Whose ox have I taken? Whose donkey have I taken? Whom have I cheated? Whom have I oppressed? From whose hand have I accepted a bribe to make me shut my eyes? If I have done any of these things, I will make it right" (1 Sam 12:3).

Fourth, practice thanksgiving day and night. Thanksgiving drives away discontentment, keeps us focused on what God is doing and has done, keeps us from attributing our success to ourselves and so is an effective antidote to pride. It keeps us from becoming the center of the universe. John Calvin said that thanksgiving is the chief exercise of godliness. It is the essential spiritual posture of the child of God, as Romans 1 suggests in contrast with the opposite, namely, that life disintegrates when we refuse to give thanks and stop revering God (Rom 1:21).

Fifth, plan on lifelong learning. The typical life, says Richard Bolles in his famous *Three Boxes of Life*, starts with twenty-five years of study, followed by forty years of work, followed by twenty years of an orgy of leisure.[26] Some older entrepreneurs go astray in their twilight years. What we need is all three all the way through—study, work and play. If we keep working, at least on some level, and keep learning and keep playing, we are more likely to end well.

Finally and ultimately, we relinquish life in this world and are left with the only treasure we can take from this life to the next. And just what is that? First, it is friendship with Jesus that we take through the valley of the shadow of death. The new heaven and new earth is characterized by continuous communion with God. That is why someone who does not want God would not want to go to heaven. But there is another treasure.

In several Scriptures there is the powerful suggestion that work we have done in this life, whether in inventing a new service or dreaming up a new product, if done with faith, hope and love, and in some way beyond our imagination, can on the return of Christ be purged of sin and transfigured to take its place in the new heaven and new earth. Our labor in the Lord is not in vain (1 Cor 15:58).

---

[26]Richard N. Bolles, *The Three Boxes of Life: And How to Get Out of Them* (Berkeley, CA: Ten Speed Press, 1981).

Work done with faith, hope and love can pass the fire test at the end (1 Cor 3:10-15).

Entrepreneurial Commission

The University of Cambridge is over eight hundred years old and situated in a fabled intellectual community with majestic buildings and spires, oozing with a high intellectual pedigree. There are many colleges and halls that compose the University of Cambridge, and one is Ridley Hall, where John Stott, among others, has studied. I (Rick) was invited to speak at a conference on Christianity and entrepreneurship in March 2009 by our friends and noted scholars in Cambridge, Richard Higginson and Peter Heslam. At the conclusion of the weekend conference all the participants assembled for a Sunday service in the chapel. Hosted by two Anglican priests, with a message delivered by a Vineyard Pastor from Florida, this disparate ecumenical gathering held a prayer and commissioning of attendees for greater effectiveness in the marketplace. This was an impactful and unique experience—one that I had never been part of previously or even seen prior to that time.

In that same spirit we offer this "Entrepreneurial Commission" as you embark on Christ-inspired entrepreneurial leadership.

Go into the marketplace, into the church, into not-for-profits and charitable organizations. Go in the power of the Holy Spirit. Go in the creativity that God the Creator continues to inspire in us. Go with the stick-to-it-ness which is the fruit of the Spirit. Go with integrity. Envision things that have never been produced before. Invent new services and products. Implement these as a way of loving your neighbors near and far. What you are doing is kingdom work—you are advancing the lovely and life-giving rule of the sovereign Christ so that the potential of God's creation is unfolded, human life is enhanced and improved, people and nations are helped. Create organizational cultures that humanize workplaces, that steward the gifts and talents of people, and that in beliefs, values and symbols express a foretaste of the new heaven and earth.

And where you have opportunity, and especially where you work, when the way you work and the organizational culture you have crafted raises the questions of why and how come, put in a good word for Jesus and the good news of the kingdom of God. You are doing the Lord's work. You are in full-time ministry. Do not love money, because you cannot serve God and mammon. But use money as a means of blessing people. Take wise risks knowing that your gracious God is inviting you so to do, and knowing that even if you fail, God can turn that failure into growth and learning. And in all things work for the glory of God. And at the end of it all, when you meet the Master of the universe, may he say, "Well done, good and faithful servant. Come and enter the joy of your Master." Forever and ever, Amen.

For Reflection and Discussion

1. What concrete ways can you contribute to the synergy of church and entrepreneur in your own context (local church, Christian organization, etc.)? What recommendations could you bring to your local church to increase the recognition of workplace ministries of entrepreneurs and other people working in the world?

2. What does "a long obedience in the same direction" mean to you?

3. How do you answer Walter Wright's questions: (1) What is the most important thing in your life right now (and do not quickly say "God")? (2) What do you want your life to be about? (3) At this point in your life what do you want to learn next?

4. Who knows how much you make and what you do with it? Does this matter?

Mini Bible Study. In the chapter we visited the final speech of Samuel in 1 Samuel 12:1-25 as a contrast with Solomon's end. Read how Solomon was (and we are) supposed to function in leadership in Deuteronomy 17:14-20. What clues do we have that would enable us to finish well?

Entrepreneurial Leaders Organization

The vision of the Entrepreneurial Leaders Organization (ELO) is to be the leading entity to equip, connect and inspire Christian entrepreneurial leaders for difference-making worldwide. ELO works through a joint initiative with the World Evangelical Alliance, an organization that represents 600 million Christians globally.

ELO is directed by Richard J. Goossen, and supported by an international board of advisors comprising successful practitioners from a range of industries. ELO is also supported by an esteemed network of thought leaders and conference speakers from institutions such as McGill, Oxford, Cambridge, Yale, Baylor, Thunderbird Graduate School of Management and Regent College.

ELO engages in three activities. First, Goossen engages in frequent speaking on topics related to Christians in the marketplace, business as calling and faith at work. Goossen has spoken at business conferences, churches and academic institutions around the world. His presentations incorporate the work of ELO. Second, ELO engages in extensive academic research on the topic of Christian entrepreneurial leadership. Goossen, in collaboration with students and professors, has conducted over three hundred in-depth interviews with Christian entrepreneurs. The partial output of this research includes five books of collected interviews, which have been published under the title *Entrepreneurial Leaders: Reflections on Faith at Work*. Third, ELO organizes Entrepreneurial Leaders Conferences, which are widely recognized as the leading events of their kind. ELO has held annual conferences for seven years with a live event in Vancouver that is attended by approximately five hundred individuals from around the globe. ELO also works with host partners to have videocasts in other locations.

The work of ELO is propelled by the desire of Christian entrepreneurs and business people to receive executive-level training, to meet like-minded peers and to be constantly reinspired for greater difference-making in the marketplace and beyond.

For further information please see www.eleaders.org.